Leading with
PEOPLE

Leading *with* PEOPLE

A Six Pillar Framework for Fruitful Leadership

Zac Bauermaster

ConnectEDD Publishing
Hanover, Pennsylvania

This publication is available at discount pricing when purchased in quantity for educational purposes, promotions, or fundraisers. For inquiries and details, contact the publisher at: info@connecteddpublishing.com

Published by ConnectEDD Publishing LLC
Hanover, PA
www.connecteddpublishing.com

Cover Design: Kheila Casas

Leading with PEOPLE by Zac Bauermaster. —1st ed.

Paperback ISBN 979-8-9874184-9-9

Praise for *Leading with PEOPLE*

Nourishment for the soul through compassion, wisdom, and hope! With personal stories, scripture, and practical advice, Zac Bauermaster empowers us to break free from living a distracted life and fulfill our purpose. *Leading with PEOPLE* serves as a compass, guiding us to prioritize what truly matters—a life centered around God and people. This book has the potential to transform not only how we lead, but also how we live. A must-read for those with a heart for God and a heart for people.

> —Lainie Rowell | Bestselling author, award-winning educator, and TEDx speaker

In *Leading with PEOPLE*, Zac teaches us to hold on to the true purpose of leadership. We prioritize the trust and hearts of others, while lifting and empowering our teachers, staff, and community. In these challenging times, we must lead with love and have faith, no matter the odds. This book and the pillars Zac shares are a must-read and the guide for leading the next generation.

> —Salome Thomas-EL, Ed.D. | Award-winning Principal, Teacher, Author, and Speaker

If you enjoyed Zac Bauremaster's first book, *Leading with a Humble Heart: A 40-Day Devotional for Leaders*, you will love *Leading with PEOPLE: A Six Pillar Framework for Fruitful Leadership*. With compelling vulnerability, Zac tells his story of struggle, recovery, and growth in life and leadership—allowing readers to walk alongside him while inviting you to apply lessons learned. Whereas faith-driven leaders found Zac's first book a resource for personal devotion, this book is perfect for either individual or group book study. Zac fills each chapter with inspiring stories—from charming and contemporary to historical and scriptural. Do not put it down until you've read to the very end, where he provides 49 days of targeted actions for applying the six pillar principles. While reading this book, I cried often, laughed frequently, and thought deeply. I believe you will also be equally inspired, challenged, and encouraged by this book.

—William D. Parker | Principal Matters, LLC, Founder. Educator, Author, Speaker, and Host of *Principal Matters: The School Leader's Podcast*

Readers will find a vulnerable and relatable journey in Zac Bauermaster's book *Leading with PEOPLE*. His personal experiences, coupled with his unique P.E.O.P.L.E. structure, provide a framework for any leader to discover new ideas and revisit fundamentals in a powerful read that is filled with heart—a heart focused on God's leadership and timeless wisdom as the touchstone for anyone looking to be an effective leader and follower.

—Amy P. Kelly | Author, Keynote Speaker, and Vice President of Consulting, The Jon Gordon Companies

Leading with PEOPLE uses humor and practical wisdom to help you see leadership through the lens of compassion. As the owner of a private practice, Zac opened my eyes to a counter-cultural, yet powerful, type of leadership. He uses storytelling and humble transparency to guide the reader through a hands-on, biblical, and effective approach to leading and loving others.

—Heidi Scott | Owner of Morning Star Counseling, LLC

Personal vulnerability and liberal use of supporting Scripture are the hallmarks of Zac's writing. Aspiring and veteran leaders alike will find this book to be both helpful and encouraging.

—Roger North | Founder/CEO North Group Consultants

This generation is looking for leadership that demonstrates emotional intelligence—characteristics such as humility, perspective, courage, and people skills. We gain insight, inspiration, and encouragement for our own journeys when leaders are vulnerable and share their learnings from lived experiences, struggles, and outcomes. Zac Bauermaster does not hold back from sharing personal stories, fears and failures, his base of faith, and his intentionality in seeking help from others. Chapter by chapter in *Leading with People*, Zac builds the case for a framework that will aid aspiring, emerging, or growing leaders who strive to continually improve. Give his Action Plan a try—through its daily activities, you will gain courage, practice humility, and share perspectives with others. More importantly, though, you will move beyond leading to *Leading with PEOPLE!*

—Melanie Deppen | Executive Director, Grace Leadership Institute
     A Ministry of Grace Church, Erie, Pennsylvania

Leading with PEOPLE: A Six Pillar Framework for Fruitful Leadership is a delightful read that offers a simple, yet value-packed, guide for the Christian leader who desires to create a more positive work environment, build stronger relationships, and achieve greater success for the glory of God."

—Ahna Fulmer | CEO, Early Morning Habit™

Leading with PEOPLE is a remarkable book that beautifully combines faith and leadership. The author's emphasis on prioritizing, empathizing, observing, praying for and with, loving, and encouraging the people we lead resonates deeply. This book challenges us to move beyond self-centered leadership and embrace a humble, compassionate approach that truly makes a difference in the lives of others. With its authentic stories, scripture verses, and practical application, *Leading with PEOPLE* is a must-read for anyone seeking to lead with faith and impact.

—Alfonso Mendoza | Host of the *EdTech Life Podcast*

Leading with PEOPLE: A Six Pillar Framework for Fruitful Leadership is a remarkable and insightful guide for anyone seeking to excel in the realm of leadership. In his book, Zac provides a comprehensive framework that offers invaluable wisdom for leaders in various fields. What sets this book apart is its emphasis on people. These six pillars are not just theoretical concepts but practical principles that can be applied in real-life leadership scenarios. I particularly appreciate Zac's emphasis on the human element of leadership. In today's fast-paced world, it's easy to forget that leadership is fundamentally about people, and this book serves as a timely reminder. I highly recommend this book to aspiring and seasoned leaders alike. It is a powerful resource that will inspire and equip you to become a more effective and compassionate leader, capable of achieving fruitful outcomes in your leadership journey.

> —Dr. Rachel Edoho-Eket | School Principal and Author of *The Principal's* Journey: Navigating the Path to School Leadership

I love this book! In *Leading with PEOPLE*, Zac provides significant insights into leading with greater success, fulfillment, and purpose. Practical, applicable, and inspirational—three of my favorite qualities in any book. *Leading with PEOPLE* is a mix of beautifully written narratives and direct solutions any leader can apply immediately.

> —Kelly Croy | Director of Innovation & Instruction for Port Clinton City Schools, Host of *The Wired Educator Podcast*, Author

If you're passionate about loving and leading others, Zac Bauermaster's book, *Leading with PEOPLE*, is one you've gotta check out. Great insights and biblical views on what leading with people is all about!

> —Coach Kurt Hines, Head Coach Coronado High School Football, Teacher, and Keynote Speaker

Titles don't make leaders, actions do. *In Leading with PEOPLE*, Zac provides exactly that: an actionable framework to fruitfully lead others in our homes, schools, businesses, and organizations. Through personal stories that will move you to tears and laughter often, scripture, and research, Zac reminds us to keep it simple in leadership—love God and love people. *Leading with PEOPLE* opens our eyes to the importance of having others walk alongside us in our leadership roles while simultaneously walking alongside others. This book will transform your leadership.

> —Jonathan Alsheimer | Teacher, Speaker, Author of *Next Level Teaching*

Through clarity, humility, and prayer, Zac provides a solid framework as a guide for all leaders to understand leadership better, validate what they knew all along, or recalibrate their leadership style to meet the needs of today. He takes some critical principles of the Bible and makes them applicable for more significant impact and influence but with a much-needed emphasis on leading oneself first. Regardless of one's title or rank, this is a must-read.

> —Dwight Carter | Educational Leader

I found Zac's book to be a profound blend of inspiration and practical wisdom. In *Leading with PEOPLE*, Zac emphasizes the importance of nurturing our relationship with God as the foundation for all others. Through the use of verses, songs, prayers, and real-life examples, Zac's words resonate deeply, guiding readers to align their hearts with God's purpose. This book not only inspires but equips, providing practical insights that ensure a strong foundation for leading with people. It's a truly tremendous read that will leave you with the tools and motivation to lead with both purpose and compassion.

> —Dr. Tracey C. Jones | Tremendous Leadership, T3 Solutions, Inc.

Leading with PEOPLE is the book I didn't know I needed. Zac Bauermaster does a fantastic job weaving actionable steps with stories and biblical principles. I can't wait to use some of the many things I learned from reading this book, and I know this is a book I'll be sharing with others time and time again.

—Todd Nesloney | Director of Culture and Strategic Leadership at TEPSA, speaker, and author

Written at the perfect time, *Leading with People* isn't just a book—it›s a paradigm shift. Seamlessly weaving scripture with the tangible experiences of leadership, it challenges us to redefine our notions of influence and power. Delving deep into the PEOPLE framework, this blueprint emphasizes the pillars of *Prioritize, Empathize, Observe, Pray, Love,* and *Encourage.* Each chapter beckons leaders to journey alongside those they lead, championing a leadership style rooted in humility, connection, and genuine care. The thoughtfully placed "Pause and Take a Deep Breath" sections are a testament to the book's commitment to introspection and personal growth. Whether you're a seasoned leader or just starting your leadership journey, this book serves as a beacon, underscoring the profound truth that true leadership is not about leading *over* people, but *with* them. Embark on this transformative journey and see leadership through a lens of compassion, collaboration, and heartfelt connection.

—Thomas C. Murray | Director of Innovation, Future Ready Schools® Best-Selling Author of *Personal & Authentic & Learning Transformed* Washington, D.C.

What an *excellent book!* If you desperately want to make a positive impact in the world around you, and if you are eager for God to equip you and use you to enhance the lives of others, this book will show you the way. *Leading with PEOPLE* provides a beautiful framework for biblical leadership. Vulnerably written, it is very engaging while also thoroughly biblical; it is incredibly inspiring while also practically helpful. What is written here will aid you in taking your vertical relationship with God and extending it horizontally to the people you have the privilege to lead and serve. I heartily and joyfully recommend it for your good and for the good of all those in your sphere of influence!"

—Craig Allen Cooper | USA Today Best-Selling Author
of *Glad You're Here: Two Unlikely Friends Breaking Bread and Fences*, co-written with Walker Hayes (2022), and Author of *Overflowing Mercies: 100 Meditations on the Tender Heart of God* (2024)

Dedication

To my favorite people:

Carly, you make me better—I love you.
Olivia, Eliot, and Issac, as you journey through life,
keep it simple: love God and love people.

And remember...

Who builds a boat with no clouds in sight?
Who walks up to a giant and picks the fight?
Who turns a lion's den into a petting zoo?
Who can have a church in the fire of furnace? Well, I'll tell you who

Crazy people trust in Jesus
Following Him wherever He leads us
Kingdom seekers, walk by faith believers
Here's the church, here's the steeple, here's to all God's crazy people

-Crazy People, by Casting Crowns

Table of Contents

Introduction

"Zac...Zac...Zac, can you hear us?" As I regained consciousness, I knew exactly what was happening–it was a fear of mine playing out in reality. I was sitting at my desk at school, my head inside my arms as I leaned forward with my head on the desk. Only minutes before, I led a team meeting across the hallway in the science classroom. As I came to consciousness in my 7th-grade social studies classroom, I was surrounded by teachers, the school nurse, and the assistant principal. I had never felt so vulnerable and exposed. My hidden story was playing out for others to see, and I knew I wouldn't be able to hide this struggle of mine much longer. I had just publicly passed out. This struggle was something I was trying to hide–something I thought I was going to snap out of any day now. Similar events had happened before, but never in a public setting. I was embarrassed–I was supposed to have it all together, and now I would have to share things about myself I would prefer to keep hidden.

I slowly sat up at my desk, surrounded by a team of *people* as they circled around me. I didn't realize at the time just how much that moment would begin to change my perspective of six simple letters: P, E, O, P, L, E. When I found the strength (I never felt weaker than at that moment), I walked with the nurse to her office along with my brother-in-law, a teacher in the same building. They walked side-by-side with me to ensure I didn't fall in the hallway. The nurse took my blood pressure and handed me a few snacks to help with my blood

1

sugar. Everything checked out OK, but I knew the truth; I knew how much I was struggling inside. My brother-in-law drove me home from school that morning, where I met my wife in the middle of the kitchen, held on to her, and cried.

About a half-hour later, the house was quiet as I sat down and wrote in my journal:

> *Lord, I don't understand it. Today in a meeting, the anxiety hit, and I passed out. I'm fearful–I'm fearful of how I will respond to this. I'm fearful I will never feel like myself again. But I trust you, I think I trust you, I want to trust you. You are in control; take control, Lord! I cast my anxieties and fears on you. Use me to advance your kingdom. I pray I can be a testimony for you. Show me how I can use this in my life and for the lives of others. I pray you give me words and actions as I move forward and more people know about my struggle. Take my fear; take it, Lord! I know you are molding me; give me patience, Lord; the waiting is hard. I love you, Amen!*

For about half of a year, I had been battling significant anxiety and depression (I'll go into more detail throughout the book), and I was hiding it. No one would have guessed the inner struggle I was experiencing. That night I hardly slept–anxious, fearful, uncertain of what would come my way. What would people say to me? What would they think? How should I address people? How are they going to look at me? I was embarrassed, as if I had failed, like I was falling short and couldn't handle the responsibilities in my life. As I awoke the following day, I wrote again in my journal:

> *This is the day the Lord has made! Use me today, Lord, to advance your kingdom. Give me your words today, Lord, not mine. Keep my human words far away and intercede for me, Lord Jesus. I pray those*

that hear me listen with an open heart and mind. I trust you, Lord. I am tired, I feel weak, I'm nervous, and I want you to be my champion and take all of that today! You are my champion! I know I can't do anything today without your strength…fill me, Lord, fill me! Help me advance your kingdom today. Fill my head with scriptures from above! I love you, Lord…Amen.

I didn't want that day to happen. The day I passed out at school was a day that I feared. But guess what? I'm glad it happened, and I wouldn't go back and change it for anything. What happened that day and the days to come began to transform my perspective on life and leadership–and continues impacting me daily. I never knew just how blind I was to the *people* around me. That is where *Leading with PEOPLE* begins.

The PEOPLE Framework

Leading with PEOPLE is precisely that: recognizing that to lead people effectively, we must be willing to be led ourselves. This book aims to help us rethink our daily approach by humbly remembering that leadership is about leading *with* people. How we lead says a lot about us and the One for whom we work. If you had asked me before the day I described in the opening story, I would have said leadership is about "leading people." I never thought too long about that simple four-letter word "with." It was not a word I ever thought to look up before, but when I came across the two words defining it, I realized it was perfect for leadership. The definition of "with" is "accompanied by" (Oxford Learner's Dictionaries, n.d.). We must lead "accompanied by" people.

This book focuses on two main concepts regarding leading *with* people. We can't have one without the other, and these two concepts are interwoven through various stories throughout the book. All the stories point back to the two main themes:

1. First, we will look at leading *with* people by seeing how much we need people in our lives as leaders. *We can't lead alone.* I know; I've tried. **As we lead others, we *must* lead *with* people in our lives.** To lead at our best, we must simultaneously be led while leading others.

2. Secondly, we will look at leading *with* people by breaking down the six pillars of the PEOPLE Framework. PEOPLE is an acronym with six components to guide your daily leadership, no matter where you're leading from and who you are leading. *PEOPLE* stands for: Prioritize, Empathize, Observe, Pray, Love, and Encourage. **As we lead others, we *must* lead *with* Prioritizing, Empathizing, Observing, Praying for and with, Loving, and Encouraging the people we lead.**

Leading with People is for leaders from any walk of life with a heart for God and a heart for people. This book is about leading *with* people in ALL areas of life and involves our thoughts, words, and actions—every second of every day no matter our leadership role. *Leading with PEOPLE* is about quiet, humble leadership in life's big moments and life's mundane moments. There's no more trying to lead ourselves—we must lead *with* people.

While there are plenty of distractions wanting to pull us from what matters most, let's allow our mission to drive the way we approach every day: prioritizing people, empathizing with people, observing and meeting the needs of people, praying for people, loving people, and encouraging people. **It's the people who make a place special.** The first chapter lays the foundation for the PEOPLE framework. Chapters 2 through 7 focus on a specific pillar of the framework. Chapter 8 provides a 49-day, 7 x 7 *Leading with PEOPLE* Action Plan designed to walk you through humbly leading *with* people day by day. Chapter 9 concludes the book with a prayer for leaders. Each chapter includes a key pillar, authentic stories, scripture verses, and application.

You can implement the action plan in different areas of your life at different times. You may need to work through the action plan focusing on your family. Others may navigate the action plan focusing on people at work. Some of you may implement pieces of the action plan simultaneously at work and at home. You may have a struggling relationship in your life or a relationship you are looking to strengthen. Focus the entire plan on that person. It could be your spouse, a child, or a close friend. The plan is all about being intentional in our relationships–*with* God and *with* people.

Leading with PEOPLE is an invitation for leaders to let go of control and lead humbly and confidently, recognizing we need people in our lives walking alongside us as we lead and walk alongside others. Lastly, and most importantly, our primary responsibility as leaders is obedience to God. There's no better example for us to look at than Jesus, who lived out thirty-three years on earth in obedience to his Father as he served the people around him every step of the way.

Pause and Take a Deep Breath

You will find "Pause and Take a Deep Breath" sections throughout the book. Before every Sunday morning service begins, my pastor encourages the congregation to "pause and take a deep breath." He knows that many of us are either coming into the service struggling to be still, thinking about events or interactions from the past week, something that occurred that morning, or looking ahead to what is on the schedule for the coming week. It's hard to be still and in the moment; it's hard to slow down. Our minds are constantly pulled to regrets of the past or worries of the future, and we miss the present. The "Pause and Take a Deep Breath" sections of the book are designed for you to do just that: literally pause, take a deep breath, and remember God's goodness in that specific moment. They may be reflections, Bible verses, or questions to ponder. The intent is not for you to speed through this book. The purpose is for you to take your time, examining your relationship with God and your relationship with others to help you grow as a leader and grow in your relationships. These sections are designed to encourage you as you journey through these pages of the book and, more importantly, journey through life and leadership. So when you see a "Pause and Take a Deep Breath" section, don't skip over it. I promise: you and the people you lead will be better for it.

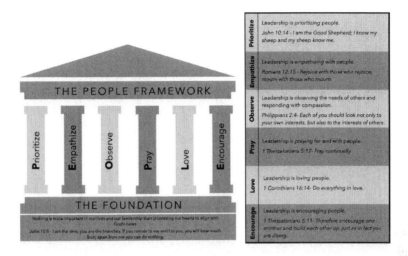

The PEOPLE Foundation - Nothing is more important in our lives and our leadership than prioritizing our hearts to align with God's heart. "I am the vine; you are the branches. If you remain in me and I in you, you will bear much fruit; apart from me you can do nothing." -John 15:5

Pillar #1 - Prioritize

Leadership is prioritizing people.

John 10:14 - I am the Good Shepherd; I know my sheep and my sheep know me.

Pillar #2 - Empathize

Leadership is empathizing with people.

Romans 12:15 - Rejoice with those who rejoice; mourn with those who mourn.

Pillar #3- Observe

Leadership is observing the needs of others and responding with compassion.

Philippians 2: 4 - Each of you should look not only to your own interests, but also to the interests of others.

Pillar #4 - Pray

Leadership is praying for and with people.

1 Thessalonians 5:17- Pray continually.

Pillar #5 - Love

Leadership is loving people.

1 Corinthians 16:14 - Do everything in love.

Pillar #6 - Encourage:

Leadership is encouraging people.

1 Thessalonians 5:11 - Therefore encourage one another and build each other up, just as in fact you are doing.

CHAPTER 1

The Foundation

Nothing is more important in our lives and our leadership
than prioritizing our hearts to align with God's heart.
"I am the vine; you are the branches. If you remain in me
and I in you, you will bear much fruit; apart from
me you can do nothing."

-John 15:5

"Out of all the staff members in this school, you are the last person I would have expected to hear is going through such difficulties," my principal said. It was early in the morning, the day after I passed out at work, when I entered my principal's office to provide him a glimpse into my story. I was struggling; I was struggling badly. But as my principal stated, no one would have guessed.

I remember coming across a news article about an elementary school forced to evacuate due to an engineer notifying the district of structural concerns. As a safety precaution, the faculty and students evacuated the building and relocated to another district facility. Weeks prior, there were growing concerns over the increase in cracks found in the building, but a structural engineer deemed it safe for occupancy. However, after further investigation into the structural integrity of the building, the same engineer notified the district of a concern, prompting the evacuation.

Here are a few of the structural engineer's observations of the school building:

+ The building was not designed in conformance with the code requirements at the time of construction.
+ Serious design flaws led to growing cracks in window piers, corridor walls, and classroom partition walls.
+ Masonry piers were not reinforced.
+ The building was not designed to resist seismic loading.

Here's the thing: from the outside, this was a beautiful elementary school building, reasonably new, and everything seemed just fine. But on the inside, there was a completely different story.

That's exactly how I felt the day I passed out at school while leading a meeting:

1. I appeared to have it all together on the outside.
2. "Cracks in my walls" were growing on the inside and had been growing for years. I realized I had been trying to cover them up.
3. The day I publicly passed out was like the day the school was forced to evacuate. My "building" needed to be repaired, and I couldn't carry the load anymore.

A Foundation Matters

Gallup conducted a study from 2005 to 2008 exploring *"why people follow."* During the study, Gallup asked a random sampling of 10,000 followers, "What leader has the most *positive* influence in your daily life" (Rath and Conchie, 2008)? The participants were asked to write down three words that best described the leader's contribution to their life. The research team collected the open-ended responses and found distinct patterns.

One of the emerging themes or basic needs from the study noted by participants was *stability*. People want to know their leader will provide them with a solid foundation. Additional words mentioned around the theme of stability were security, strength, support, and peace. Participants "reported that the best leaders were the ones they could always count on in times of need" (Rath and Conchie, 2008).

Pause and Take a Deep Breath

How about you? What leader has the most positive influence on your daily life? What three words best describe the leader's contribution to your life? If you're able, reach out to that leader to say thank you for their leadership.

This chapter is the foundation of the PEOPLE Framework as it sets the stage for leading ourselves effectively to lead others fruitfully. More specifically, this chapter focuses on building and maintaining our foundation as leaders. A foundation is "the lowest load-bearing part of a building, typically below ground level" (Oxford Learner's Dictionaries, n.d.). A foundation provides stability–for us and for those we lead.

Leadership is challenging–a heavy lift and a tremendous responsibility. Leaders carry the weight for many people daily. We can't cut corners when it comes to leading ourselves. Much like the school described in the opening of this chapter, if we take shortcuts in building our foundation, we won't withstand the weight of leadership. Structural integrity is one of the most critical concepts in engineering and construction. A structure can hold together under a load, including its weight, without breaking or deforming excessively.

If we don't operate with structural integrity, it's only a matter of time until it leads to structural failure. Structural failure is the "loss of the load-carrying capacity of a component or member within a structure or of the structure itself" (Your Dictionary, n.d). Structural failure typically happens when something is stressed beyond its strength limit. Although structural failure often looks like a single factor causes it, it's most likely a combination of factors. That's what I discovered in my life: structural failure due to various factors. As I began to unpack the structural failures in my foundation and began my "repairing," I learned many valuable lessons from and *with* the people around me. Let's begin.

A Foundation Like David

In 1 Samuel 16, God told Samuel, "I am sending you to Jesse of Bethlehem. I have chosen one of his sons to be king" (1 Samuel 16:1). When Samuel arrived, he saw Jesse's son Eliab and believed he was the one who would be Israel's next king: "Surely the Lord's anointed stands before the Lord" (I Samuel 16:6). But the Lord said to Samuel, "Do not consider his appearance or his height, for I have rejected him. The Lord does not look at the things man looks at. Man looks at the outward appearance, but the Lord looks at the heart" (I Samuel 16:7).

After looking at Jesse's sons, Samuel asked, "Are these all the sons you have" (1 Samuel 16:11)? Jesse responded, "There is still the youngest, but he is tending the sheep" (1 Samuel 16:11). By outward appearances, David's brothers seemed to be a better choice to be the next King of Israel, but David was the one. When King Saul acted foolishly, Samuel told him, "The Lord has sought a man after his own heart and appointed him leader of his people" (1 Samuel 13:14). Luke says in Acts 13:22 says, "I have found David, son of Jesse, a man after my own heart." Even though David wasn't as tall, old, or handsome as his brothers, *he was a man after God's own heart*. Where did David get his heart? From spending time with the Lord in the shepherd fields as he tended to the sheep.

Aligning Our Hearts with God's Heart

"Zac, where's your heart right now?" Shortly after I opened up about my struggles, this powerful question from a mentor caused me to reflect deeply on my heart. Honestly, I had never thought much about my heart and its impact on my life. I was going through the motions of life and didn't realize the structural failure occurring at my foundation. Like structural failure, I failed to see I was stressed beyond my strength limit. In my struggles and weakness, my mentor challenged me to examine and pour my heart out to God. Paul Tripp (2021) describes the significance of the heart wonderfully:

> If we take all the ways the Bible talks about this word, the Bible describes the heart as the control center of your personhood; it's the center of your thoughts, it's the center of your desires, it's the center of your emotions, it's the center of your purposes and your motivation. And so, the father is saying, This is what drives you, this is what controls you, this is what shapes your living. You have got to be concerned about your heart.

Our hearts are the foundation of who we are. Much like our hearts, a foundation is not something we typically see, yet it is the "load-bearing" part of who we are and how we lead daily. It's not the people and situations that cause us to speak and respond as we do; the people and situations that allow our hearts to express themselves. I learned that to lay my foundation and provide stability, I must prioritize myself first. We fruitfully prioritize ourselves by prioritizing our heart as the foundation of who we are—*following* God by remaining rooted in His word and prayer. Jesus says in John 15:5, " I am the vine; you are the branches. If you remain in me and I in you, you will bear much fruit; apart from me you can do nothing." Jeremiah uses the analogy of a tree planted by the water to describe being rooted in God to live fruitful lives:

> Blessed is the one who trusts in the Lord, whose confidence is in him. He will be like a tree planted by the water that sends out its roots by the stream. It does not fear when heat comes; its leaves are always green. It has no worries in a year of drought and never fails to bear fruit. Jeremiah 17: 7-8

Guess what? Heat will come in life and leadership, and we certainly experience drought. However, when we root ourselves in the vine and send out our roots "by the stream," we will never fail to bear fruit in the lives of the people we lead, no matter how challenging things may seem. We must follow before we lead, thus prioritizing our hearts to align with God so that we can care about the things God cares about and fruitfully lead others. The world will often tell us to follow our hearts, but that can be dangerous advice as our human hearts can easily deceive us. Jeremiah says, "The heart is deceitful above all things" (Jeremiah 17:9). We want God to create in us "a pure heart" (Psalm 51:10). Instead of following our hearts, we should follow God's heart and allow Him to shape our hearts to align with His.

A verse I pray to God often is Psalm 139: 23-24: "Search me O' God and know my heart, test me and know my anxious thoughts. See if there is any offensive way in me and lead me in the way everlasting." This prayer from David is the perfect prayer for us as we aim to align our hearts with God's heart. David knew that we cannot know our hearts at the depth God knows them, so he would ask God to discern his actions and motives. As my mentor shared with me, we want to "pour out your hearts to him" (Psalm 68:2).

Pause and Take a Deep Breath

Pour out your heart to God with the following prayer: *"Search me, O' God, and know my heart, test me, and know my anxious thoughts. See if there is any offensive way in me and lead me in the way everlasting."* Where is your heart today?

As leaders, we always want to pause and think, "Where's my heart in this?" There has to be a heart behind it, but our hearts must be in the right spot aligned with God's heart to lead others fruitfully. Next, we will look at three critical applications for building and strengthening our hearts as the foundation of who we are, helping us see the importance of aligning our hearts with God's to have a fruitful impact on the people around us:

> As leaders, we always want to pause and think, "Where's my heart in this?"

1. Treasure
2. The Bare Word of God,
3. Prayer

Treasure

Sitting in church one Sunday morning, I heard my pastor ask the congregation, "What's your treasure?" Similar to the question my mentor asked me about my heart, that question hit me hard. Matthew 6:21 tells us, *"For where your treasure is, there your heart will be also."* Treasure is a "valuable object" and is to be "kept carefully" (Oxford Learner's Dictionaries, n.d.). That treasure may be the desire for human praise, success, achievements, money, financial security, or comfort and ease—earthy treasures battle to fill our hearts every day. When we allow those earthly treasures to take hold of our lives, our actions follow. What we treasure organizes our time, finances, words, and actions.

Never Enough

My wife and oldest daughter took a long weekend trip to Florida, so I took my two youngest kids to Baltimore for an overnight trip. We stayed at a hotel, went out to eat multiple times, went to the National Aquarium, and bought lots and lots of candy! It was an enjoyable trip, and a fun fact: I love candy. I remember standing at Baltimore Inner Harbor after buying the kids candy at the local CVS when both started complaining. I thought, "I have given them whatever they wanted this entire trip, and they're still complaining!" Then I told them, "It's never enough, is it? No matter what I give you, you always want something else. It's just never enough."

As the last words, "It's just never enough," came out of my mouth, I paused with conviction. How often could God say those exact words to me, "Zac, it's never enough, is it? No matter what I provide for you, you always want something else; it's just never enough." When we allow things of this world to be our treasure, that's precisely how we'll feel: like it's never enough. Whether it be success, education, money, a job, status, fitness, food, entertainment, or even our relationships. If we make them our treasure, our treasure chest will be left empty. When we make Jesus our treasure, only He can satisfy us. As Paul said in 1 Timothy 6, "Godliness with contentment is great gain. For we brought nothing into this world, and we can take nothing out of it (v. 6 and 7). We can only be truly content when our hearts are rooted in Jesus, and one does not have to live with an itch for more.

Pause and Take a Deep Breath

My wife has a sign next to our coffee maker that reads, "Less is more unless it's coffee." How have you found less to be more in your life? Has desiring more and having more left you feeling empty?

Meaningless, Meaningless

In the book of Ecclesiastes, Solomon reflects on a time when he lived apart from God, chasing idols and materialism. He begins the first chapter describing life from his human perspective, "Meaningless! Meaningless!" says the Teacher. "Utterly meaningless! Everything is meaningless." Throughout the short book of the Bible, he shares that life is meaningless apart from a relationship with the Lord. He discovered that power, prestige, and pleasure don't fully satisfy. Only through God can we experience purpose, true joy, satisfaction, and fulfillment.

The song "Graves to Gardens" by Brandon Lake and Elevation Worship (2020) starts with the following four lines echoing the words found in Ecclesiastes:

I searched the world
But it couldn't fill me
Man's empty praise
And treasures that fade
Are never enough

I know when I'm making Jesus my treasure in life and when I'm not. The chorus in the song, "Turn Your Eyes Upon Jesus" (Lemmel, 1922), is a convicting reminder for me and what I treasure in my life:

Turn your eyes upon Jesus
Look full in his wonderful face
And the things of earth will grow strangely dim
In the light of his glory and grace

When my eyes aren't fixed on Jesus as my treasure, things in this world seem bright and important, ultimately leading me to live distracted, for myself, my wants, and my desires. When I'm in the Word of God, in prayer, walking closely alongside others, things of this world grow strangely dim. Hebrews 12 reminds us to fix our eyes on Jesus, the author, and perfector of the faith.

What treasures are most valuable to you? How do you see those treasures impact your daily leadership—the way you organize your time, interact with others, and the actions that follow? What's hindering you as you run the race God has marked out for you?

Pause and Take a Deep Breath

When you fix your eyes on Jesus and your heart aligns with God's, you can live each day with great encouragement to faithfully live out your mission.

Where are you fixing your eyes today? Are things of this world bright and distracting you from being a man or woman after God's own heart?

The Bare Word of God

Aren't the things we tend to remember amazing? Whether song lyrics from twenty years ago or statistics of our favorite athletes, we tend to remember some not-so-important stuff. I was recently driving with my family when a song I hadn't heard for many years came on. Guess what? I "impressed" my kids by singing every word. Sometimes, what gets stuck in our brains can be downright annoying. Do you ever get frustrated by what you know and think, "Why do I even know that?" For fun, the song I sang for my family in the car was a rap song from Kris Kross called "I Missed the Bus."

My mom always said, "Garbage in, garbage out." She meant to be careful of what I was consuming with my eyes and ears. As Luke 6:45 says, "A good man brings good things out of the good stored up in his heart, and an evil man brings out the evil in his heart." When I was a teenager, I had some inappropriate songs on CDs, and my mom would find them and break them right in front of me. We were even driving down the highway once when she took one of my CDs and threw it like a frisbee out of the window (I knew that wasn't a good time to talk with her about the problem with littering). She knew whether I was trying it or not, those lyrics would become ingrained in my mind. Unfortunately, I can still recite every lyric to some of those songs.

As my mom was equipping me as I grew up, she knew I needed something useful in my brain and, ultimately, in my heart. She would write Bible verses on 3 x 5 index cards and leave them by my nightstand. I keep those scripture-filled index cards by my bed today as they grow more and more relevant daily. She wanted me to hide those verses in my heart so I was equipped for whatever would come my way-something I could use no matter the situation or setting. She knew the importance of memorizing something that would change my life and point others to Jesus through my interactions. She was equipping me to have wisdom from God at my disposal every moment of every day. Similarly, my dad tells my family, "Be in the word, memorize it, continually recite it to yourself throughout the day."

Pause and Take a Deep Breath

Get what matters most stuck in your head, the Bare Word of God. The Bible is transformational; the scriptures allow God to perform surgery on our hearts to transform us from the inside out to be more like Jesus and align our hearts to God's heart.

Power of Prayer

Leadership can be all-consuming. Actually, leadership *is* all-consuming. It's filled with responsibilities, pressures, busyness, and increased demands. When asked about his plans for the upcoming day, Martin Luther said, "I have so much to do that I have to spend the first three hours in prayer" (Luther, n.d.). This line by Luther is a paradox we should all consider. Our days are so busy, yet there is One who holds the day in His hands and wants to spend one-on-one time with us. Jesus set the perfect example for all of us. Jesus knew pressure, busyness, and challenges should drive us towards prayer, not away from it, and he set the perfect example of how we should prioritize prayer. Mark 1:35 says, "Early in the morning while it was still dark, Jesus got up, left the house, and went off to a solitary place, where he prayed."

Jesus purposefully set aside time to talk to God. He prioritized being alone with God for the first part of his waking hours. Before the day-to-day responsibilities began, Jesus spent time with his Heavenly Father in solitude, pouring out His heart. He put himself in an environment where he could entirely focus on God. We also see throughout the Bible how Jesus would withdraw from large crowds and find a solitary place to pray (Luke 5:16). Jesus would regularly retreat from the world to restore himself through His heavenly Father before returning to the daily tasks and needs of others.

Pause and Take a Deep Breath

How can you be purposeful in refreshing yourself through prayer by retreating from the day-to-day to replenish and rejuvenate your leadership? What causes you to neglect prayer?

Foundation in Action

Pray Continually

The quiet, still time with Jesus is an essential part of life. Busyness often looks and feels like productivity, but busyness keeps us from what matters most: Jesus and people. With all the people we interact with daily and the things that come our way, it's easy to prioritize lesser things. The early morning hours with the Lord are refreshing. We need to continue to prioritize early mornings in prayer, not just in the morning but throughout the day, to quiet our hearts and mind to focus on Jesus and align our hearts with God's heart.

Take Action

As we look to build and strengthen our foundation, focus on the two words found in 1 Thessalonians 5:17, "pray continually." Not only by praying in the morning but, as the verse says, "continually." Pray throughout the day. Prayer is an ongoing conversation with God. Feel free to set multiple alarms on your phone as a reminder to pray. And don't worry about praying the perfect prayer; there's no such thing. Open your heart to God, praying for strength, wisdom, guidance, and discernment in your leadership journey. Ask Him what you should pray for as you humbly pray (John 15:5), *"You are the vine, I am the branch, apart from you I can do nothing, but in you I can bear much fruit. Help me bear fruit, I need you, I can't do it on my own."*

As Jesus tells us in Matthew, "Ask and it will be given to you: seek and you will find; knock and the door will be opened to you. For everyone who asks receives; he who seeks finds; and to him who knocks, the door will be opened (v. 7-8). God doesn't promise this life will be easy, but He promises He is right there with us every step of the way. Pray.

Heart Surgery

R.C. Sproul said, "The word of God can be in the mind without being in the heart, but it cannot be in the heart without first being in the mind" (Sproul, n.d.). Simply put, we need to be in the word of God daily for heart transformation; we need to prioritize spending time in the scriptures, memorizing scripture, and living out scripture. James 1:22 says, "Do not merely listen to the word, and so deceive yourselves. Do what it says." We need to know the heart of God, and He reveals His heart to us in the scriptures.

Cody Carnes' (2019) song, "Run to the Father," says: "My heart needs a surgeon, my soul needs a friend, so I'll run to the Father again and again." We must keep running to the Father through His word so the great surgeon can perform surgery on our hearts. The word is alive and active (Hebrews 4:12) and will strengthen us in leadership no matter what comes our way.

Take Action

In addition to praying, commit to memorizing scripture and make studying God's word part of your daily routine. Begin with Bible verses or passages that are meaningful to you, the season of life you're in, the situation you're facing, or an area with which you're struggling. I don't know what you're going through or what God is preparing you for in your leadership, but find a verse that hits close to home in your season of life. As you begin to memorize verses, it's not about quantity, but quality. Take your time as you fill your heart with God's wisdom. As you learn a verse, study the passage's context as well. What is the meaning behind the verse?

Write the Bible verse on a slip of paper and keep it in your pocket as a reminder throughout the day. As Paul says in Philippians, "Finally, brothers, whatever is *true*, whatever is *right*, whatever is *pure*, whatever is *noble*, whatever is *lovely*, whatever is *admirable*—if anything is *excellent* or *praiseworthy*—think about such things" (Philippians 4:8). Filling your heart and mind with those words described by Paul comes from reading the Bare Word of God. God's word is a lamp to your feet and light for your path (Psalm 119:105).

Heavenly Treasure

Earthly treasures distract us from our heavenly treasure and hinder us from living and leading fruitfully. Jesus says in Matthew 6, verses 19-20, there are only two kinds of treasure: earthly treasures and treasures in heaven. We want to ensure that our only treasure is our Heavenly Father and we seek first His kingdom and righteousness (Matthew 6:33). When asked what the greatest commandment is, Jesus replied, "Love the Lord your God with all your heart and with all your soul and with all your mind. This is the first and greatest commandment" (Matthew 22:37-38). When we make God our treasure, our hearts align with His, and we can treasure what God treasures. When we treasure the things God cares about, we can be His hands and His feet as we lead and serve others, as our time, words, and actions follow accordingly. When our hearts align with God's heart, we take the vertical relationship with our Heavenly Father and overflow to the people in our life.

> When we treasure the things God cares about, we can be His hands and His feet as we lead and serve others, as our time, words, and actions follow accordingly.

Take Action

Spend quiet time journaling a list of the current treasures in your life. Who or what treasure are you seeking? Examine your heart and note how the treasures you list impact your daily life. Be honest in your reflections. Do the treasures help you run the race God has marked out for you? Or do they get in the way of being more like Jesus? Remember, your heart will follow what you treasure and overflow in how you treat others. For where your treasure is, there your heart will be also (Matthew 6:21). In Jesus is where you find your worth, your identity.

Don't Fight Your Battles Alone

We're not made to walk through our lives and our leadership journeys alone. My wife told me once, "You are human; you can't do it all yourself; quit trying to." As a husband, father, teacher, and coach, I thought I had to hold it all together. I failed to see how much I needed people in my life. I quickly learned that many people were ready to fight my battle with me, which lightened my load immensely.

> God puts people along our path because we need them, and they need us.

We are made to be in community with one another. We need people in our lives. We need to live and lead *with* people. God puts people along our path because we need them, and they need us. Maybe this is an excellent time to pause and send that person or those people a message thanking them for their impact on your life. Be specific in your message.

Jesus didn't send his disciples out alone; he "sent them two by two" (Luke 10:1). The disciples' work was hard—they faced many challenges and hardships. They couldn't walk this earth alone. The Lord designed people to be interdependent—with Him and others. Unfortunately, like me, we often experience the illusion of independence, that we can do life independently. We are to live humble, interdependent lives with other people. The Teacher writes in Ecclesiastes 4 that "Two are better than one, because they have a good return for their labor. If either of them falls down, one can help the other up. But pity anyone who falls, and has no one to help them up" (v. 9 & 10).

A mentor challenged me to reflect on who was coming with me in my battle with anxiety and depression. He encouraged me to identify a group of friends and family members to bring along on my journey. My struggles opened my eyes to how much I needed others in my life as part of my foundation. I realized I needed daily help from people walking alongside me.

Take Action

Reflect on who you can surround yourself with as part of your foundation. Focus your prayer on who you can seek out as a mentor in your life. Ask God to bring someone into your life who would be willing to invest in you. Is there someone you can mentor? They may already be right in front of you. Not only seek to bring a mentor into your life but commit to mentoring someone else. The timing may not be right at the present moment, but keep your eyes open. Reach out to those people and open up. "As iron sharpens iron, so one man sharpens another" (Proverbs 27:17). We can find comfort in peace in not fighting our battles alone. The battles belong to the Lord. Don't fight your battles alone. Joshua had Moses; Elisha had Elijah; Timothy had Paul; who's coming with you?

Lead from Overflow

Many people immerse themselves in more activities than their calendar can hold, and life becomes one big shuttle from one commitment to the next. They feel the more involved they are, the more worth they have. We don't want to wait until it's too late and realize in our busyness that we missed what's most important: our relationship with God and the people in our lives. Not only that, we don't want to lead from an empty cup with nothing left to pour out to others. Reflecting on my struggle with anxiety and depression, I was operating far less than my best, over-committed, and trying to do too much. To overcommit means (Merriam Webster, n.d.):

1. To obligate (someone, such as oneself) beyond the ability of fulfillment
2. To allocate (resources) in excess of the capacity for replenishment

That's exactly what I was doing. I was living out the definitions of overcommitment:

1. I was obligating myself beyond the ability of my fulfillment.
2. I was allocating in excess the capacity for replenishment.

Instead, we should lead from overflow (Collins Dictionary, n.d.):

1. To flow over or across; flood.
2. To flow over the brim or edge of.

Leaders must take the time to reflect on when we are operating at our best. Instead of leading from a place of overcommitment, leaders must lead from overflow. We've heard it said repeatedly in many ways: the first person we must lead is ourselves. We can't fruitfully lead others if we're not leading ourselves. Leaders must model leading themselves well and lead others to do the same. We don't want to find ourselves and the people we lead overcommitted. Lastly, and most importantly, ask God to fill your cup so you can overflow into the lives of others.

Take Action

Reflect on when you are living and leading at your best. Create a T-chart; at the top of one column, write "Overcommitted." On the top of the other column, write "Overflow." Next, create a list under each column of when you are leading from a place of overcommitment and when you're leading from a place of overflow. Commit to building your foundation under the items listed under "Overflow." I need to remember to go back to the basics: eating healthy, exercising, getting quality sleep, reading, quality time with my family, spending time outdoors, keeping my phone and other distractions away, and prioritizing the early morning hours for prayer and scripture reading.

Use the following bullet points as a guide:

+ When do you feel and operate at your best?
+ What rejuvenates you, and what drains you?
+ Who are the people who rejuvenate you, and who are the people who drain you?
+ What do you need to say no to?
+ What must you say yes to?

Step Out of Your Comfort Zone

My high school basketball coach would enter us in summer leagues to help our team grow and improve for the upcoming season. All the local high school teams would join the same summer league at a local high school within the county, where they would play against one another throughout the summer. It was a summer league comprised of rural and suburban school districts. Our coach entered us in that league for a few years before making a change. One summer, he entered us into a summer league about an hour away in the city of Coatesville, Pennsylvania. I remember we all pulled up to the basketball courts with our eyes wide and jaws dropped for the first game. This league was different. The league was played outdoors in the middle of the city and comprised mainly of adult teams. The teams were bigger than us, faster than us, stronger than us, and in an area not familiar to us.

Why did my coach enter us in that league? Because it stretched us outside of our comfort zone—it made us better. We could have stayed in our little county playing against teams our age, the same size, the same speed, and the same strength. Once the regular high school season began, he would write "Coatesville" on the whiteboard before games to remind us of our work over the summer. That experience helped me see that growth and improvement don't occur inside our comfort zones.

As I continued through my struggles, I learned how much I needed people as part of my foundation. That meant stepping out of my comfort zone and opening up to others. Opening up to others is not something that comes naturally to me. Leading with people stretches us beyond our comforts, helps us grow, and connects us with others. Much like my high school basketball team's summer league and the impact on my team's regular season, when I began to step outside my comfort zone, talk with others, and share my struggles, I felt the growth begin to occur, and the foundation strengthen. It felt as if immediately my base was strengthened. Not only that, but I also started to see people differently. *Leading with People* will stretch you outside your comfort zone. That's a good thing—outside your comfort zone is where growth occurs.

Take Action

Identify a comfort zone holding you back from maximizing your God-given gifts and abilities. Additionally, prepare to step outside your comfort zone as you work your way through this book. Create a list of doubts and fears currently consuming brain space. Is it something as "simple" as opening up to a trusted friend about something in your life? Find a quiet space to listen to the song "No Longer Slaves" by Bethel Music (Case, J., Helser, J., Johnson, B., 2015). Turn each of those doubts and fears into prayer and ask God to fill you with His confidence, not your own. Rip the list up and throw it out. God is bigger than all of your fears and doubts. Step out of your doubts and fears and step into your calling. Where is God calling you to step outside your comfort zone? Turn it over to Him.

Rest in God's Provisions

Not only did Jesus live this pattern of retreating and reentering by himself, but he also taught his disciples the same pattern of withdrawing from crowds before entering back in. In Mark 6, the apostles had returned from ministry and gathered around Jesus to share all they had done and taught. So many people continued to come and go that Jesus said to them, "Come with me yourselves to a quiet place and get some rest" (v. 30-31).

God blesses our work and rest. We need rest to operate at peak efficiency with the gifts and talents God has given us. The world will tell us that we must always work and get ahead, which couldn't be further from the truth. I have pushed myself but quickly realized it is not sustainable for my job, health, or family. David says in Psalm 62, "Find rest, O my soul, in God alone; he is my fortress, I will not be shaken" (v. 5). A person who will not rest lacks trust in God's provision. On the flip side, rest shows trust in God's provision.

Take Action

Rest, quietness, stillness, and trust are beautiful words. This "action" item may be the hardest for you: simply being still, resting in God's provisions. David said in Psalm 23, "The Lord is my shepherd, I shall not be in want. He makes me lie down in green pastures, he leads me beside quiet waters" (v. 1-2). Lie down in those green pastures, and walk beside those quiet waters; God is your shepherd, and you have all you need. Rest in what God has done for you, is doing for you, and will do for you; He is in control. Take a deep breath and picture Jesus saying to you, "Come to me _____, you are weary and burdened, I will give you rest."

Summary

Jesus says in Matthew 5:24-27:

Therefore, everyone who hears these words of mine and puts them into practice is like a wise man who built his house on the rock. The rain came down, the streams rose, and the winds blew and beat against that house; yet it did not fall, because it had its foundation on the rock. But everyone who hears these words of mine and does not put them into practice is like a foolish man who built his house on sand. The rain came down, the streams rose, and the winds blew and beat against that house, and it fell with a great crash.

The two houses described by Jesus looked the same on the outside but had two completely different foundations. The real foundation of our lives is usually hidden and exposed when the storms of life come our way. As we face the challenges of life and leadership, rain will come, floodwaters will rise, and the wind will swirl; what foundation are you standing on? The rock or on the sand?

Once we lay the foundation, we can begin building our first pillar of the PEOPLE Framework. It's important to emphasize that we can't add pillars without first laying our foundation; there would be no stability; the pillars of PEOPLE would not stand. As Zig Ziglar said, "You don't build a business. You build people, and the people build the business" (Ziglar, n.d.). It's time for leaders to take action and set the example of "building people." I want to close the opening chapter with one question: *As you prepare to lead yourself and lead others, where's your heart right now?*

CHAPTER 2

Prioritize

Pillar #1 - Leadership is *prioritizing* people.
"I am the Good Shepherd; I know my sheep and my sheep know me."

John 10:14

"It's not about you." Those four words hit me hard. My sister had recommended the book *Purpose Driven Life* by Rick Warren (2002), and I was met by those four words to start the book. When I was hit with anxiety and passed out at school, that wasn't a finish line like I had made it out to be in my head. Instead, I realized it was a starting line. It's funny how the exact situations we try hardest to avoid are the ones that end up benefiting us the most. As we saw in the last chapter, it was a starting line to opening my heart and eyes to the people around me. Those four words, *it's not about you*, were exactly right; this life is not about me. We are made by God and for God. My pastor often says, "A barometer of our relationship with God is how we treat people."

Let me be honest with you, that doesn't mean leading with people is easy; it takes effort and intentionality, and I need to work on it daily. Prioritizing people doesn't come naturally to me; I'm a constant work in progress. I often still struggle. Thankfully, I am surrounded by people in my life who are part of my foundation. They are honest with me and help to refocus me when I need it. As I continued reading the *Purpose Driven Life*, I read the line, "Focusing on ourselves will never reveal our life's purpose" (Warren, 2002). As I began working on this chapter and the topic of prioritizing people, my wife, Carly, told me exactly what I needed to hear (although not what I *wanted* to hear).

It was early on a Saturday morning, and we sat on the couch beside one another. I knew things were off and tried to make small talk. Have you ever tried that? You know a relationship is struggling, and you attempt to start talking about the most random things with really no purpose behind it. I brought up schedules, our calendars, and the kids to try and get conversation going. As I expected, it went nowhere. It was spring, and things had been busier as the end of the school year was winding down. We were coaching our daughters' softball and son's baseball teams. It was a season of constantly being on the go.

After a few minutes of my failed small talk, Carly did what she does best, speaking honestly and directly with me. She began with, "I guess I'll go ahead and start the real conversation. We don't have anything to say because we're drifting apart," she said. She added, "You don't always practice what you preach, and we're (the family) the byproduct of it. I'm tired of it."

Ouch. As always, she was right. She knew it, and I knew it, yet this wasn't the first time she had to have a similar conversation like this with me. I've struggled to prioritize other people in my life. About a year and a half before this conversation, we had a similar discussion–again, on a Saturday morning.

I headed home from work one Friday evening exhausted, realizing I had missed getting home for dinner with my family six out of the past eight days. As I headed home, I was looking forward to resting and being with my family, but also making time to get work done. However, as I spoke to Carly on Friday evening, she said she did not want to see my laptop out that weekend. Carly is wise and knew my pace was not sustainable, and I was beginning to stretch myself too thin. I listened to her, but deep down inside; I knew there were a few things I "needed" to do.

I wouldn't say this is the smartest thing I've ever done, but I woke up early Saturday morning to get out my laptop and work. Unfortunately, (or fortunately, however, you want to look at it) Carly also woke up early that day and came into the living room area to find me working on my laptop. She gave me a quick look, but the intelligent man I was at that moment continued to work. Carly continued with her morning routine and headed downstairs to work out.

As I continued to work upstairs at the kitchen table, my oldest daughter, age nine, woke up and came out to sit on the couch. I felt the pressure at that point. There was "just one more thing" I needed to finish, and I would go sit with my daughter on the couch. I had a "busy" week and did not see my kids nearly as much as I should have. Carly returned upstairs to find my daughter sitting on the couch alone and me at the table, continuing to scramble to finish a few work items on my laptop. She shot me a glare before sitting down with our daughter.

Finally, as I got up from the table and spoke to Carly, I could tell she was having none of it, and rightfully so. I told her that "I just needed to finish" a few things and would be all in for the rest of the weekend. She stopped, told me to listen to myself, and told me that for a few months now, I had been saying, "*I just need to finish*" or "*There's one more thing I need to do.*" She shared that is the same reason I headed to work early each morning and stayed late each day—because I had this to-do list that always had "one more thing" or something that "I just need to finish."

Knowing I was not in a good spot, I followed my wife into the room, and she dropped some profound wisdom on me. She said, "Zac, look around. What do you see?" Now to set the stage, Carly was a stay-at-home mom at the time with our three young kids, ages nine, six, and four. As I peered around the room, I saw a pile of laundry, clothes needing ironing, toys on the floor, and other tasks still requiring completion. She said, "Do you know what would suffer if I always focused on just needing to finish one more thing all the time?" I humbly paused and listened. "The relationships with the kids and our relationship would suffer. There will always be something that still needs to be done, whether at work or home. *But when our daughter wakes up, and you continue to work, you show her and our family what you prioritize and what is most important to you.*"

Those lines hit me hard but were accurate based on my recent choices. I had always prided myself in being people first, but *that morning I realized how much I was putting a to-do list before people*–people I cared about, my wife and kids. I realized I had fallen into the same pattern at work, focusing on getting work done rather than entirely investing in people and relationships as I should have been. It's not *what* we have time for, but *who* we

> It's not *what* we have time for, but *who* we make time for.

make time for. How often do we waste time and energy on things that don't really matter? It's not until we hit life-altering conversations or moments that we realize loving God and loving people are what matter most. The way I spent my time showed what I valued most, and it was not people. I knew I needed to return to my core values and prioritize people at home and work.

Prioritize People

My wife was right. You're probably thinking, "You can say that again." So I will: *My wife was right.* Through various seasons I have made my family a byproduct of my work. I have also made the people in my life and at work a byproduct of my work. I preach prioritizing people, specifically leading my family first, but that doesn't mean I've mastered it, and I'm not sure I ever will. Quite frankly, I struggle with it. Carly accurately told me I was making our family a byproduct of my life. A byproduct is a secondary, sometimes unexpected or unintended result (Merriam-Webster n.d). That word *unintended* hits me. We don't set out to make our spouses, children, or people in our lives secondary to everything else we're doing, but much like my struggles, they can quickly become a byproduct without us even realizing it. That's not what I want my family to be and it's not what I want the people I lead to be. Too often, people in my life have become a byproduct of my hurried pace and to-do list nature of life and work, causing me to miss out on the people in my life. How about you? Do you want people to be a byproduct in your life, a secondary result, unintended but inevitably produced by prioritizing something else over them?

I had the privilege of meeting the legendary football coach, Tony Dungy, when he was the keynote speaker at a mentorship event. Dungy shared some of the best advice he ever received from his coach and mentor, Chuck Noll. Dungy shared that the first thing Coach Noll said to the team was:

> "Men, I want to welcome you to the National Football League. You're now going to be paid to play football, so that makes it your profession. But don't make football your whole life. If you make football your whole life, you're going to be disappointed."

Most importantly, Coach Dungy shared that not only did Coach Noll emphasize the saying, "Don't make football your whole life," he modeled it and lived it out daily. We need to take that same mentality in our life and leadership.

When we take the vertical relationship with our Heavenly Father and spread it horizontally to the people we lead, we lead with a heart that *prioritizes people*. We want to lead with a heart that *prioritizes* people, not a heart that puts ourselves first, making people a byproduct. Contrary to a byproduct, a priority is something or someone we put ahead of something else and is regarded or treated as more important than something else. As leaders, it's a non-negotiable, we must prioritize people, whether in our homes or outside the home. As Coach Dungy said, "When we lose sight of people, we lose sight of the very purpose of leadership" (Dungy & Whitaker, 2011).

Pause and Take a Deep Breath

Is there something in your life or work that you are making the treasure of your life, and you know it's impacting the people around you? Fill in the blanks for yourself. Don't make _____ your whole life. Then, model it. We can't have people, specifically those closest to us, be byproducts of our work and daily tasks. *As leaders, we need to practice what we preach.* As Coach Noll said, if we make _____ our whole life, we are going to be disappointed. I would add: "and the people around us will be disappointed."

Prioritizing People Builds Trust

A second basic need emerging from Gallup's *why people follow* study was *trust* (Rath & Conchie, 2008). The 10,000 participants cited words such as honesty, integrity, and respect to best describe a leader with the most positive influence in their daily life. These words "are the outcomes of strong relationships built on trust" (Rath & Conchie, 2008). The basic need for trust is built by prioritizing people one relationship at a time. To trust their leader, people have to know their leader and desire for their leader to know them. If we want to connect with people, we can never forget how important it is to work at it daily. Relationships require time and effort—we must be intentional with our relationships. Trust is the one thing that changes everything (Covey, 2008).

> If we want to connect with people, we can never forget how important it is to work at it daily.

Prioritize Like the Good Shepherd

There's no better example of prioritizing people than Jesus. Jesus' entire ministry on earth was relational, prioritizing people every step of the way. I love how Jesus refers to himself as the good shepherd in John 10. A shepherd is protective and firm but gentle, proactive, and wise. Ultimately, we see in John 10:11 that Jesus says, "I am the good shepherd. The good shepherd lays down his life for the sheep."

Shepherding leadership comes from the heart and is a desire to serve others. It begins with treasuring Jesus as our Good Shepherd. To serve others effectively, leaders must prioritize getting to know people.

We can look at how a shepherd and leadership correlate in many ways, but this chapter will focus on the relational aspect of leading like a shepherd. Jesus says in John 10:14: I am the good shepherd; I know my sheep and the sheep know me. Not only does Jesus say that He knows his sheep, but he also says, "My sheep know me." Like Jesus as the Good Shepherd, leaders must take the time to get to know those they lead while at the same time allowing others to get to know them. People desire authentic leaders, leaders who personally invest in those they lead. Of course, we will never know the hearts of others like Jesus does, but we can follow his example of having a heart for people. Shepherds lead by relationship, and the relationship is where trust is built.

While leading an entire flock, the shepherd knows that although the sheep may all look and appear the same, the flock is actually composed of individual sheep with unique personalities and characteristics.

Knowing those we lead as unique individuals within the larger group is essential. A shepherd prioritizes the individual relationships with those they lead and who are entrusted to their care. As leaders, we must professionally and personally uncover every individual's skills and interests. What motivates them, and what are their likes, dislikes, goals, and aspirations? How about their family and personal hobbies? Leaders must engage with people, asking questions regularly with their eyes and ears open.

Prioritize in Action

Prioritize with a Name

One of my favorite shows is *King of Queens*, with Kevin James and Leah Remini, better known as Doug and Carrie in the show. In one episode, "Name Dropper," there is a scene in which Doug is at a work event for his wife, Carrie. Doug is terrible with names and doesn't want to be at the event whatsoever. Carrie stays close to him all evening to ensure he doesn't do or say anything stupid. Doug also has a fear of not remembering names. The evening is almost over, and they are ready to go home when Carrie needs to step away and use the restroom. Seconds after she leaves, one of her colleagues waves and comes over to talk to Doug. Immediately, he gets nervous and begins rambling because he can't remember her name. The conversation is coming to a close when Doug's father-in-law, Arthur, walks over and says, "Douglas, aren't you going to introduce me?" Doug doesn't remember her name and fumbles around for a few seconds. So what does he do? He did what any of us would do. He grabs his chest and fakes a heart attack. The scene concludes with Doug in an ambulance on the way to the hospital.

This scene in *King of Queens* is certainly exaggerated and all in good humor. But it is a fun example of how much we hate to forget or not know someone's name. I feel much more confident heading into a situation or conversation when I know a person's name. I can't stand it when I don't know or forget someone's name. Instead of engaging in a conversation, sometimes I attempt to avoid the person or conversation. I can only imagine how much that has a detrimental effect on the relationship.

The founder of Chick-fil-A, S. Truett Cathy, always maintained that he wasn't in the chicken business but the people business. One of the ways he exemplified people first in how he led his restaurant business was by knowing his customers by name (Greenway, 2015). Dale Carnegie famously said, "A person's name is to him or her the sweetest or most important sound in any language" (Carnegie, 1936). Knowing a person's name and calling them by name is a leadership game-changer. Remembering someone's name and using it shows a greater connection to who that person is. Using a person's name shows intentionality, value, and respect. It shows you care. How can you be intentional about learning names and calling people by name?

In Luke 19, Zacchaeus was a hated, wealthy chief tax collector who wanted a better view of Jesus as he entered and passed through Jericho, so he climbed up into a sycamore tree above the crowds gathering below. When Jesus reached the crowd, he looked up into the sycamore tree and said, "Zacchaeus, come down immediately. I must stay at your house today" (Luke 19:5). Notice the first word out of Jesus' mouth, the chief tax collector's name, "Zacchaeus." Jesus knew the importance of a person's name. I can only imagine how Zacchaeus felt when he heard his name come out of Jesus' mouth. "Wait, what? Jesus knows my name, a little tax collector everyone hates; he knows me?"

Similarly, Mary Magdalene wept at the tomb after Jesus' crucifixion because the tomb was empty and the stone was rolled away (John 20:11). When she was crying at the empty tomb, she turned and saw Jesus standing there but didn't realize that it was him. Jesus asked her why she was crying and who she was looking for. Thinking he was the gardener, Mary said to him, "Sir, if you have carried him away, tell me where you have put him, and I will get him" (John 20: 15). Jesus responded with one word, her name, "Mary." Jesus revealed Himself to Mary by telling her who she was to Him, not by telling Mary who He was. John 10:3 says, "He (Jesus) calls his own sheep by name."

Take Action

Strive to show people you genuinely care for them by calling them by name. Do this, remembering that God has called *you* by name; you are His (Isaiah 43:1). Whether face-to-face, on the phone, by email, or by text message, put in a little extra effort by prioritizing using the person's name. It's just a little thing that can go a big way.

Do you struggle with names? Focus on being intentional with learning names. Try a few of these suggestions:

1. Be confident–change the mindset of "I'm bad with names."
2. When you meet someone, actually pause and listen to their name. How often do we forget a person's name one second after hearing them say it because we weren't actually listening?
3. Repeat someone's name back to them sparingly throughout a conversation after meeting them.
4. Make name associations in your head to draw on connections as you meet someone.
5. If you forget a name, don't allow the awkwardness to continue. Say something like, "Can you tell me your name one more time, please?"

Prioritize with a Greeting

I'm sure you've heard the famous quote from Maya Angelou, "At the end of the day, people won't remember what you said or did; they will remember how you made them feel" (n.d). One morning when serving as an assistant principal, I talked to my building principal about how early my kids wake up. I explained how I enjoy waking early to focus on a few things I like to complete before the rest of the house wakes up. I was transparent and told him I'll hear little footsteps coming and, for a second, think, "Ah, I'm not ready for them to be up." Instead of greeting my kids with a warm morning welcome, too many times, I treat them like an interruption. As my principal almost always did, he responded with a story.

He shared that when he was young, he would always wake up early and go out and sit on the living room couch, much like my daughter. One of his most vivid childhood memories is his grandfather coming over, saying good morning, and greeting him with a hug and a kiss on the forehead. He remembers his grandfather sitting on the couch with him and being in his presence. He doesn't remember everything they talked about, but he remembers his grandpa, stopping whatever he was doing and greeting him each morning. It made him feel like the most important person in the world. Do you have anyone in your life like that—someone who makes you feel like the most important person in the world by how they greet you? He shared that those interactions with his grandfather have always impacted how he greets others, his own family, and the families within his school. I remember watching him give a building tour to new families of the school, his eyes would light up, and his passion shined through as he welcomed families and showed them around. He told me welcoming new students and families was one of his favorite parts of his job. "You can't ever get a first impression back," he said. "Make it a good one."

I attended an event called "The Men of Iron 27:17 Dinner" as a guest to celebrate what God was doing in a mentorship program called *Men of Iron*. The organization's mission is to "change a culture, one man at a time," with Proverbs 27:17 as its core verse. As a few friends and I headed into this large event, we were met by someone who greeted and welcomed us at the door. I didn't think much of it and thought he was someone they had assigned as a greeter, but I appreciated the warm welcome.

About an hour later, after finishing dinner, a few speakers began to share. The individual who greeted us at the door, Travis, was one of those speakers. As he spoke, you could feel his passion for people and the work that he does. His presentation was filled with pictures of people surrounding him along his journey and how much they meant to him. As we left the event, guess who was at the door interacting with guests as they headed home? Travis, the same guy who greeted and welcomed us on the way in. He thanked us for coming with a handshake and a smile as he sent us on our way.

Those two interactions caused me to reflect on the impact of greeting others. Travis didn't know me, my friends, or most of the people at the event, but he prioritized us by how he greeted us. He didn't have to stand at the door greeting people that evening; it wasn't his job requirement or an assigned duty for the night; he chose to do it on his own, and his actions did not go unnoticed. Much like my principal's grandfather, he made the time to greet others intentionally. We can have a significant impact no matter where or who we're leading by how we greet others.

How often do we have opportunities to lead in our homes or work by the way we greet people and send them off for the day?

How do you greet your family when they wake up or when you return home at the end of a long

> We can have a significant impact no matter where or who we're leading by how we greet others.

day? How do you greet people at work: in the hallways, by the copier, or when they stop by your office? Is your head down, ready to accomplish the next thing on your list? Are you showing you care about them and they are important to you? Or are you treating them like an interruption?

Take Action

Be purposeful in how you greet others. Make people feel special by the way you greet them. It could be something as simple as a handshake, fist bump, or a smile at work. Maybe it's a kiss or hug to your family members as they wake up or you arrive home from work. It doesn't have to be a grand gesture. Show people you are grateful they are in your life by putting a little extra effort into how you greet them. Remember, people won't always remember what you said or did, but they will remember how you made them feel (Angelou, n.d). Take pride in how you greet others—it matters.

Prioritize Putting Your Phone Down

"Dad, why do you love your phone so much?" Ouch. I almost didn't put that line in the book because I was so embarrassed. My eight-year-old daughter and I were practicing softball outside when I needed to run into the house to grab something. On the way, I tapped my phone on the counter and saw I had a notification. I opened my phone and began to respond to the message. Before I knew it, a few minutes passed, and I was completely distracted. Waiting for me outside, my daughter entered the house looking for me. She saw me leaning over the counter with my eyes glued to my phone and asked those nine painful words, *"Dad, why do you love your phone so much?"* Have you ever been there? Maybe you haven't been asked those exact words, but is someone in your life thinking that? Unfortunately, I have a strong inkling that I am not the only one who struggles with this.

A few weeks later, I was in the lobby of the dentist's office. The office had just opened for the day, and there were three of us in the waiting room. It was a quiet waiting room with no music; you could hear a pin drop. I sat in a chair, looking around; another gentleman stood nearby waiting for his name to be called, and a woman sat to my right, scrolling her phone. The dental hygienist opened the door and entered the lobby, ready to call one of us back. She said, "Beth," loudly. No one moved. She then repeated Beth twice, "Beth, Beth." Still no movement. There we sat in a quiet waiting room with only three people and one Beth. I knew I wasn't Beth, and the man to my left didn't look like he was Beth either. The hygienist moved closer to the woman in the waiting room and said, "Beth," this time with more of a question mark behind it. Finally, Beth's eyes popped up from her phone as she said, "Oh, sorry, I didn't hear you!"

Phones are distracting. Whether we like to admit it, we've all probably been there. We've seen videos of people texting or on their phones, running into people or objects as they move from one place to another, completely distracted. Here's another embarrassing story for you. I took my kids to a local amusement park, and as I got out of the car, I responded to a message on my phone. After spending hours at the amusement park and returning to my car, I realized the car was still running. It had been running the entire time we were at the park.

Similarly, I was running in Cape May, New Jersey, one August morning when I noticed a beautiful sunrise above the Atlantic Ocean. I stopped running, took out my phone, and attempted to capture a sunrise picture. There were even dolphins jumping in the ocean below the rising sun! No matter how hard I tried, I could not capture a picture

> **Presence is a superpower that very few of us have.**

to do the sunrise justice. Guess what? Before I knew it, I missed the real-time beauty of the sunrise while trying to take a picture of it.

Presence is a superpower that very few of us have. Are you missing precious people and moments around you? Put your phone down and look up throughout the day.

Don't Miss "The Moment"

In 1998, the Chicago Bulls were down by one point in the NBA Championship against the Utah Jazz. Michael Jordan had just stolen the ball from the great Karl Malone and had the ball with Byron Russel covering him closely as the clock ticked toward zero. Jordan dribbled toward the foul line with his right hand, crossed over to his left, and pulled up for a last-second jump shot. There's an iconic photo (captured by Fernando Medina) of "The Shot" in which Jordan is in the air shooting the basketball, as three Utah Jazz players watch the ball's trajectory nearby. Behind the backboard is a crowd of people in the stands watching intently, their eyes glued to the ball to see if the shot will go in. Everyone in the crowd is standing, mouths hanging open, a few arms in the air—but ALL eyes are on that shot. Nothing could distract those fans from missing that shot, that moment, in real-time.

Comparatively, in 2022, Lebron James was two points shy of breaking Kareem Abdul Jabaar's NBA scoring record. A photographer (Andrew D. Bernstein) captured Lebron's record-breaking basket against the Oklahoma City Thunder. Similar to the shot from Michael Jordan for the Championship in 1998, the ball is leaving Lebron's hands as two defenders look on. The crowd fills the photo's background as they look on from the stands behind the backboard. Here comes the big difference. All but one (Nike founder Phil Knight) person in the crowd has their phone out to try and capture the moment. They are not watching the record-breaking moment live on the basketball court; instead, the crowd is seen watching the moment through the little screens on their phone.

Side by side, these photos tell a story. I'm sure some fans captured an incredible video or picture on their phone, but most failed to be in the moment. Look, I recognize there were no smartphones when Michael Jordan took his shot in the 1998 NBA Finals, but every person was present, in the moment. Much like my sunrise run on the beach, the comment from my daughter, or Beth in the waiting room at the dentist, instead of staying in the moment right in front of me, I distract myself from the moment, causing me to ultimately miss it. How often do we do that to the people in our lives? We miss the "little" moments. We fail to be fully present with them and are pulled to something else—often something at our fingertips. When we do that, we fail to prioritize them, and they quickly become a byproduct. We need to be where our feet are, present and fully engaged with the people we lead.

Take Action

Commit to being where your feet are. Put your phone down and look up for the "little" moments. Be intentional about being present with the people right in front of you. Phones can connect us with people far away, but if we're not careful, phones have the potential to distance us from the people right in front of us. Don't allow your phone to pull you from the people directly in your presence. Commit to not only putting your phone down but putting it away. You don't want to miss the precious people and moments around you. Be purposeful in prioritizing the "little" moments you wouldn't have typically noticed with your eyes glued to your phone. Take a "little moment" walk with your eyes and ears attentive to your surroundings. *Be where your feet are,* present and fully engaged with the people you lead.

Prioritize Healthy People

A few months after my church hired a new pastor, he and I discussed leadership. He had a military background and shared what he learned regarding mission, vision, and tactics and how he envisioned applying that to the church. The mission is the ultimate daily goal of our church—an important assignment carried out by everyone in the church. The vision is what things look like as the mission is carried out, and the tactics are the carefully planned strategies to make the mission and, ultimately, the vision a reality.

As we continued talking, he spoke of various pillars of the vision: youth group, children's ministry, worship service, Sunday School, and so on. Then he shared a pillar that I had not thought much about: healthy people. He shared, "We can't live out our mission and carry out our vision if the church's people are trying to do too much, burnt out, and not operating at their best. We need the people of our church to be healthy."

His statement was spot on yet often overlooked in families, schools, businesses, and organizations. How often do we craft our mission statements and create our vision but exhaust ourselves and our people attempting to live out the mission? That's not a healthy culture for anyone and often leads to increased stress, anxiety, and burnout, causing individuals and the collective whole to function at levels far less than their best. Often the best way we can prioritize people is by ensuring we strive to keep them healthy to live a life in which they are engaged in their work and satisfied in their personal lives and vice versa. Leadership is not always about what we do but also what we don't do.

> How often do we craft our mission statements and create our vision but exhaust ourselves and our people attempting to live out the mission?

Early in my leadership journey, I thought working hard meant working all the time. That couldn't have been further from the truth. I sent emails at all hours of the day, including on weekends. At the time, I didn't realize what a poor example of leadership I was setting for my family and the people at work. I thought I was modeling hard work, and people would appreciate that I was always available and working. Talk about unhealthy. I quickly learned that was certainly not the case.

An example of modeling what it means when we speak of "healthy people" is prioritizing families–caring about each person as a human being, a mom, a dad, a parent, and a friend–not just an employee. A family culture of healthy people shows our families that we lead them first and invest in our homes. A culture of healthy people is knowing when there is too much on someone's plate and not spreading people too thin. In the last chapter, we looked at leading from overflow or over-commitment. Is your family or organization overcommitted to too many things? Leading with healthy people is knowing when it's good to say yes, but even better to say no. Prioritizing people emphasizes leading people to live and lead a life where they can work and live at their best. We can't carry out our mission and vision if we and the people we lead aren't healthy. Do you care about each person you work with as a human being, a mom, a dad, a parent, and a friend and not just an employee?

A school principal shared with me two meaningful compliments they had received as a leader. They may seem small, but they are impactful. The principal spoke with a teacher at her end-of-the-year evaluative meeting when the teacher shared a comment her husband made. He told her that he noticed she was working less in the evenings, her laptop wasn't open as much, she was getting to bed earlier, and she was functioning at a higher level. She added, "You know what, I'm feeling more refreshed and engaged while at work!" She thanked the principal for the culture he created at the school. She shared that for the first time, she didn't feel connected to work at all times and could fully engage with her family at home.

Another staff member said, "I just want to thank you for not sending emails in the evenings or on weekends and sending fewer emails overall. I know it seems like a small thing, but it greatly impacts me as a husband and dad, allowing me to be fully present with my family in the evening." He shared that knowing the inbox is quiet puts his mind at ease in the evening and helps him prepare for each new day. The principal didn't want anyone to feel the pressure of needing to work or the pressure that someone else is working, and they should be, too. He doesn't want anything to pop into their mind that pulls them away from being present with people. It's a small way to keep people healthy.

We want family and workplace cultures of healthy people. There's enough stress and burnout around; let's prioritize our people so they can function at their best. Prioritizing a culture of healthy people shows people that we genuinely care about them as individuals. What healthy rhythm of work and life are you exemplifying for the people around you?

Take Action

Brainstorm and implement one way you can create a culture of healthy people in your home or organization. You can't live out the mission and vision of your home or organization if your people are stressed, burnt out, and operating at levels less than their best. We want our families and all the people we lead to be healthy. Take a step back and reflect: what's a barrier that you could remove to help others work towards the mission in a healthy way? What can you remove from someone's plate today? What can you say no to for yourself and for the good of others?

Prioritize Your Most Precious Crop

I received a phone call on Memorial Day 2021 that my 93-year-old grandfather didn't have much time left to live. My family and I decided to leave our town's Memorial Day celebration, packed up a few things, filled the car with gas, and headed three hours west on the Pennsylvania Turnpike to Somerset, PA, to say goodbye.

As we arrived, there were lots of hugs and tear-filled eyes. My grandfather was resting comfortably at my aunt and uncle's house. It was a place where we had many lasting memories as a family—big family meals in the garage that began with prayer while standing in a large circle, singing the Doxology together as a family, boating and swimming in the lake, and simply being in one another's presence. But here we were for a different reason. Individually and in small groups, we headed into the room to say goodbye to my grandfather. He couldn't respond, but that didn't matter—everyone just wanted to be in his presence as he neared his final breaths.

My niece shared the idea of a prayer time. About twenty-five of us gathered in a circle around the bed where my grandfather lay. We knew he was coming to the end of his days here on earth as we circled around him, holding hands with one another. The Bauermaster family loves to circle up in prayer. Those large circle prayers, hand in hand, were often led by my grandfather. We took turns praying and praising God for my grandfather's life and the example he set for all of us. I don't remember most of the words prayed that quiet afternoon, but I do remember a line prayed by my cousin about my grandfather. He thanked God for Grandpa being a humble farmer who always cared for his most precious crop, his family. Those are such powerful words of truth. Despite all of his farming,

> You must prioritize the people inside your home before leading anyone else.

my grandfather prioritized his most precious crop above all others: his family.

Despite everything you have going on, are you prioritizing your most precious crop? Your family? You must prioritize the people inside your home before leading anyone else.

Fill in the blanks below. When you come to the end of your time on earth and finish running your race, will people say:

_____ was a humble _____ who always took care of his/her most precious crop, their family.

Like Chuck Noll's advice to Tony Dungy, my grandfather was a farmer, but didn't make farming his whole life, and he modeled how to prioritize what is most important in life. Leaders must model prioritizing their families and create the conditions for others to do the same. My dad grew up a farmer in western Pennsylvania, but the farming gene didn't make it to me. But I know one thing: farming isn't easy. It involves long hours, early mornings, late nights, daily tasks to be consistently completed, weather variables, and mental and physical exhaustion. The day starts early and ends late, with plenty of tasks in between.

Here we were at the end of my grandfather's life, circling around him, hands clenched together as we prayed because, as my cousin said, despite everything my Grandpa accomplished on the farm and in his life, he was a humble man who took care of his most precious crop, his family. He invested in us, leading the way for generations to come, and there we stood by his side and side by side with one another. Shortly after arriving home, I reflected about this in my journal:

Yesterday, we drove to Somerset to say goodbye to Grandpa. We started our day with other plans but quickly knew we needed to be there. Grandpa lay frail and silent on the bed, sound asleep. It was a humbling view and a reminder that God is our strength and our human strength will fade, but

God is renewing us internally day by day. I was reminded that loving God, trusting God, and pointing others to God are all that matters. Even after 93 years, Grandpa's time on Earth seemed as if it had quickly passed. However, we can rest confidently, knowing he is being renewed internally and will spend eternity with Jesus.

I saw how important loving Jesus and setting an example for a family is and the impact we can have as we go out as disciples. I saw a family who loves the Lord. A family that weeps for Grandpa, the memories, the love, a family grieving with one another. As Silas prayed, I saw a humble farmer with his most precious crop—his family—hand in hand by his side. Most importantly, a family who, although sad, trusts God's word, trusts Jesus' resurrection, and trusts in eternity because of what Jesus did for us on the cross. God is good all the time.

Take Action

Prioritize your family. I'm going to repeat those three words. *Prioritize your family.* This could include your spouse and children, of course, but also anyone else you consider family. In a society where things at work come home, and things at home go to work, commit to devoting all your time and attention to your family. Plan a family date or maybe even a family getaway. Your family may have been so busy recently that you must prioritize slowing down and enjoying quality time together at home. Sit down at the table and enjoy a home-cooked meal, gather for a game, share some laughs, enjoy a good dessert, and get outside to do something fun and active together. Make memories with your most precious crop: your family.

Summary

Much like my wife shared in the opening story, when we put our heads down and focus on finishing "just one more thing" all the time we show the people around us what we prioritize and what is most important to us–and people quickly become a byproduct. That's not what we want. There's always going to be something pulling for our attention. As leaders, like shepherds, we must not look to our own interests but to the interests of others (Philippians 2:4). To effectively look into the interests of others, we must take the time to get to know people, their interests, goals, strengths, weaknesses, and vulnerabilities. We must prioritize people and be eager to serve (1 Peter 5:2). Whether a mom, dad, coach, business owner, friend, or colleague, shepherd leaders prioritize people. They walk alongside them, know them by name, and care for them individually. A heart for God is a heart for prioritizing people. Leadership is prioritizing people. *It's not about you.*

CHAPTER 3

Empathize

Pillar #2 - Leadership is *empathizing* with people.
"Rejoice with those who rejoice; mourn with those who mourn."

Romans 12:15

"I'm dying," I thought to myself. "I'm dying, and no one knows it." As my principal at the time shared in response to learning about some of my struggles, "You're the last person I would have expected to hear is going through these things." Everything was going as planned from the outside, and my life had always gone according to plan. I was active in sports, played college basketball, got engaged to my high school sweetheart, graduated college, earned my first teaching position, coached high school sports, got married, built a new home, had kids, and continued my education with a smile on my face. I didn't show any anxiousness on the outside, and I'm guessing I appeared laid back and as calm as can be to the people around me. Everything was just as it should be, wasn't it?

Do you remember the Zoloft commercials where they would draw a smiley face on a paper plate and hold it up in front of their face? Behind the plate was a blank look of depression. That's how I felt. I was hurting behind the smiles. This section of the book was challenging to write; it took me back to a difficult time in my life. The main reason it was so difficult was that I tried to face the battle alone. I "needed" to be strong for my wife and kids, my players, my colleagues, and the students in my class. I attempted to hide my struggles in the dark, which only worsened them.

My chest was tight, my heart hurt. The pain in my chest led to nausea in my stomach. I would awake at night, every night, with a rapid heartbeat in a cold sweat. My mind would race. As I lay awake in the middle of the night, I would question if I should call an ambulance or have my wife take me to the hospital. I didn't know what was going on—I never experienced anything like this before. I could hardly contain the pulse beating through my chest. I would be awake most of the night, waiting for the alarm to go off. All night I restlessly lay in my bed, pounding heart, nauseous, fearing the day ahead of me. In only a few hours, I would have to wake up and face the world like everything was OK once again. But on the inside, I thought I was dying, and I was the only person who knew it.

August 11th, 2014, is the day actor and comedian, Robin Williams, committed suicide. That day scared me. When I pictured Robin Williams, I saw the laughs and smiles. How could someone like Robin Williams be in such a dark space that he would take his life? Reading the articles following his death, I learned that he suffered from anxiety and depression. Seeing footage of his old interviews and movies and now reading articles of his struggles and death shook me to the core. What if that happens to me?

I feared a public breakdown, that I would end up in the emergency room with no strength left. My mind would run wild with what could happen, and I couldn't contain my thoughts. I pictured myself in a hospital gown, exhausted and weak, unable to eat, my family around me saying, "I had no idea he was going through this." I was in the same rhythm every day; I would become so exhausted from not sleeping the night before and battling anxiousness throughout the day that I would fall asleep quickly. I certainly wouldn't sleep long, but those first few hours became my favorite part of the day.

During the day, I was exhausted and couldn't wait until night when I could go to bed. It's exhausting feeling so many physical and mental symptoms throughout the day and trying to hide them. My legs were restless; my heart beat fast; I was nauseous and felt as if I could get sick at any time. I feared getting sick and passing out publicly to the point I became fixated on the possibility of that happening. As I shared in the book's opening story, the idea of passing out became one of my worst fears, and it crippled me. I wanted to avoid the possibility of passing out in public at all costs. I experienced out-of-my-body moments when I felt like I was losing touch with reality. I would forget names, where I was, or what I was doing. It started to feel as if everyone could see my anxiety and was looking right at me. The physical symptoms would build inside me, leaving me light-headed and disembodied. These moments were the worst. Throughout the day, I would have brief moments of relief from the anxiety, and I didn't want those waves to end.

I didn't know what was happening and would Google my symptoms (that's never smart, is it?). I was tense and unable to relax. Even in the moments I wasn't anxious, I soon became anxious as I worried about anxiety and waited for the awful feeling to strike again. When I wasn't anxious, I would talk myself into getting anxious. If I noticed my heart rate increasing or my palms becoming sweaty, I would think, "Here we go again. My chest will hurt, and I will get nauseous, light-headed, and sick; what if I pass out? I'm 6'3" and 240 pounds; I will create quite the embarrassing scene and expose my weakness." This daily pattern exhausted me. I went to the doctors multiple times about my chest pain, but after numerous tests, everything checked out OK. But I knew what was happening. I knew those tests would look OK.

I started to hate this daily feeling so much that I slowly began to withdraw. I withdrew from people I previously loved to be around and from things I loved to do. When my wife wanted to do something as a couple or family, I would fake sickness so I didn't have to go out in public. I always loved working out but began to stop my daily workouts because they exhausted me. I didn't have the strength and simply didn't care anymore. I was tired of fighting these awful feelings and began not caring about things I previously enjoyed. I lost interest in everything. I would pack my lunch but was never hungry throughout the day. As I sat with my colleagues at lunch, I would move the food around like I was eating but could only manage a few small bites. I was at my parents' house with my wife one day after school when my nine-month-old daughter began to walk. I remember how much I wanted to be in that moment, love the moment, but I couldn't because of how I felt, and I hated it.

I wasn't supposed to feel this way. I was supposed to have everything all together; my life was blessed. I felt a sense of embarrassment for feeling like I felt. I told myself I could just snap out of it. "Zac, you have everything going for you; there's no reason for you to feel like this." No matter how hard I tried, I couldn't escape it. The same cycle of sleepless nights, anxious days, and living in fear continued for months. My favorite part of the day was when I was so exhausted that I would immediately fall asleep at night for a few hours before awakening to the vicious cycle again. But yet, there I was, teaching and coaching, a husband and father with a smile on my face as if everything was fine on the outside. On the inside, I had nothing left to give. It wasn't so much that I wanted to die, but I got to the point where I didn't care if I did.

Empathize *with* People

Empathy has quickly become one of the top qualities of an effective leader. When a potential teaching candidate asked, "What's the number one thing you look for when hiring teachers?" I heard a school superintendent respond with one word: "Empathy." Our lives are filled with people, and people are filled with stories. When we begin with prioritizing people, we get to know them. When we take the time to get to know people, we build trust, which is paramount to increasing our approachability as leaders for others to share thoughts, feelings, concerns, and needs. Sometimes we may even understand what others are feeling before they recognize it in themselves.

When we take the vertical relationship with our Heavenly Father and spread it horizontally to the people we lead, we lead with a heart that *empathizes with* people. When we get to know others, we can better empathize with them and fruitfully lead as we know their stories.

However, leading with empathy doesn't begin when we know someone's story; leading with empathy begins when we recognize that every person has a story.

Ernst and Young, one of the world's largest professional services organizations, conducted an *Empathy in Business Survey* in 2021. The survey of more than 1,000 Americans revealed the following (McWilliams, 2021):

> leading with empathy doesn't begin when we know someone's story; leading with empathy begins when we recognize that every person has a story.

- + 89% of employees say that empathy makes for better leadership.
- + 88% believe empathetic leadership inspires workplace change.
- + 87% say empathetic leadership builds trust among employees and leaders.
- + 85% report empathetic leadership makes them more productive.
- + Over half (58%) of employees have previously left a job because they didn't feel valued by their boss.
- + Nearly half (48%) have left a job because they didn't feel like they belonged.

Leading through an empathy lens impacts how we treat and interact with people daily—whether we know their story or not. Focusing on others requires much attention to our perspective and point of view. Too often, leaders see through our lens, from our past, from our experiences, blinding us to the needs of the people we lead. Many people's opinions are based on their experiences and perceptions, causing us to miss the stories of those around us and the impact those stories have on their lives and how they function daily.

Brandon Heath's chorus from the song, "Give Me Your Eyes" (2008) summarizes the vision we need to have as leaders, leading through God's eyes:

> Give me Your eyes for just one second
> Give me Your eyes so I can see
> Everything that I keep missin'
> Give me Your love for humanity
> Give me Your arms for the broken-hearted
> The ones that are far beyond my reach
> Give me Your heart for the ones forgotten
> Give me Your eyes so I can see

Empathize Like Jesus

When I shared my struggle with a trusted friend, he pointed me to Matthew 26. Jesus knew the hour was drawing near to his death, and he was "sorrowful and troubled" (v. 37). He took three disciples with him to the Garden of Gethsemane to keep watch while he prayed. He said to the disciples, "My soul is overwhelmed with sorrow to the point of death" (v. 38). My friend said, "Zac, Jesus empathizes with you; he felt what you're feeling." David Mathis (2015) writes:

God himself has taken on our humanity in this man (Jesus). And with it, our feelings. And with them, even our sorrows. We are finite and frail. But God gave us mighty emotions. We celebrate. We grieve. We rejoice. We weep. And we do so with Jesus as one of us.

A powerful verse of empathy in the Bible can be found in two simple yet powerful words from John 35, verse 11, "Jesus wept." When Jesus learned Lazarus had died and saw Lazarus' sisters, Mary and Martha weeping, their grief and tears moved him. Jesus shared in the grief of those mourning and identified with others in their sorrow. Paul tells us in Romans 12:15 that we should "Rejoice with those who rejoice, mourn with those who mourn." Ann Voskamp (2014) perfectly describes the empathetic lens we need to take into our daily lives:

Look for the little child everyone else forgets. Look for the hunch-backed old man no one else remembers. Look for the small, broken cracks in the world, in hearts, that would be easy to walk right by—and right there, slip in a little word that grows great courage. Miracles happen in the drawing close to the little people, the least people, the lonely people, the lost people—because this is drawing close to Jesus.

We are to live and lead as God's hands and feet—celebrating, grieving, rejoicing, and weeping with one another.

Empathize in Action

Empathize Through *Your* Story

As I continued to struggle, I headed to church one Sunday morning. Battling anxiety once again, I didn't want to be there. This particular Sunday,

I was squashed in the middle of the pew. Typically, I make sure to have an aisle seat to reduce the feeling of being trapped when anxiety would strike. I always planned an escape route and this was right around the same time I had recently passed out at work. A portion of the service was devoted to congregational members sharing their testimony and what the Lord had done and was doing in their lives. I remember a man standing up front to share his story. I had known this man most of my life. He was older than me and taught Sunday school and was active in the church. As I sat crammed in the middle of the pew listening to him share, I broke down in tears—his words struck me because they were not what I expected to hear. I almost couldn't believe what I was hearing. He told us that when he was around thirty years old, he went through everything I was going through, sharing his story in a way that was almost a word-for-word account of what I was experiencing.

Even in the moment of tears and hearing the words of his testimony, for the first time in a long time, I felt a sense of peace. A feeling of relief flooded over me. I thought I was the only one who could ever have felt this way, but as I learned that day, that couldn't have been further from the truth. Even though we hadn't talked about it, I felt like there was someone who could empathize with me.

I didn't say anything to him that day, but I sought out his phone number the next morning. I thanked him for sharing his story and said I would love to get together because "I'm going through the same thing." When he shared his story at church detailing a difficult season with anxiety and depression, I immediately felt like I had someone by my side—and a feeling that things would be OK.

He came over the next evening to meet with me. I poured out my story and struggles to him. Telling his story to our church gave me the confidence to share my own story. When hiding my story, I was blind to the stories of others around me. As I began to open up about my struggles, my eyes and heart were opened to the needs and struggles of those around me. My perspective completely changed as my vulnerability connected me with others. Our stories tell others about the goodness of God.

Take Action

Pause and take a deep breath; *you have a story*. You have a story that you need to share with someone. A story that will strengthen you and the person or people you share it with. Begin by praying that God will point you to where you can share your story. Today may be the day you share your story; today may be the first step in preparing to share your story. When we share our stories, our eyes and hearts are opened to the stories around us. You'll be amazed. Don't keep your story hidden. To tell others your story is to tell of God and what He has done and is doing in your life. As you prepare to tell your story, pray and listen to Big Daddy Weave's (Beihl, B., Redmon, J., Shirk, J., Weaver, M., 2015) song, "My Story." There are too many hidden stories; share yours. Someone needs it.

Empathize by Slowing Down

Traffic lights are awesome. Actually, yellow and red lights are my favorite. Do you know why? They force us to slow down and stop. OK, I'm kidding; I'm not a fan of red or yellow lights. I don't like traffic or stop signs either. I have things to do, places I need to go. There's no time for stopping! I'm sure many of us prefer traffic lights to be green so we can get where we want to go, continuing from one thing to another. We've all been there—driving to what's next on our agenda full speed ahead when suddenly we approach a traffic light. As we approach the light, it turns from green to yellow. This is the point where usually one of two things occur.

1. Many people think a yellow light means speeding up, so we hit the gas even harder because we don't want to stop when the light turns red. We speed through the yellow light as we see it turn to red before we get completely through the intersection.

2. Others tap the brakes to slow down and prepare to decide whether it's best to stop or if there's enough time to drive through the yellow light at a slower speed.

Be honest. Do you lead like driver #1 or driver #2?

Let's examine the traffic light as it applies to our life and leadership practices. We are the car speeding down the road moving from one place to another. We don't want to slow down, and we certainly don't want to stop. A traffic light is the last thing we want to see. We don't want anyone or anything disrupting our timing, our schedule, our plan.

But guess what? The yellow light symbolizes the need for us to slow down. When we slow down, we look out for other people. When we speed up, we look out for ourselves. As we continue to speed around from point A to B, we forget to slow down and, ultimately, we miss what's around us. When we're "driving fast," people around us look blurry out of our peripheral vision, sometimes not even noticeable. As we pump the brakes and slow down, the faces of the people around us become clearer. Slowing down allows us to assess the needs of the people around us. Far too often, we speed through life. We speed through every moment of every day, focused on task completion and what is coming next. We miss the people around us when we live at such a hurried pace. They are a blur in our peripheral vision as we speed right by.

The yellow light reminds us to slow down to see the people around us more clearly. The red light symbolizes stopping. When we slow down, we are more in tune with whether we need to come to a complete stop. Picture walking in the hallway of your home, school, business, or workplace. We're often speed walking to get where we need to go. Along the way, we pass by people at a high rate of speed with possibly a quick nod or hello.

Instead, we need to purposefully walk slower, allowing our surroundings to become more clear and decide if we need to come to a complete stop.

Like driver #1 described earlier, I like green lights–I want to keep going. Yellow light? I know what that means: speed up so I don't have to stop; there's no time for stopping. We need to lead differently. Let's embrace "yellow lights." Let's look forward to slowing down and making everything around us clearer. Let's prepare to come to a complete stop. Do you know what happens when we stop at red lights? It allows others to go before us. That's leadership - putting others before ourselves. Do you know what happens when we see a yellow light and speed up? We're like an 18-wheel tractor-trailer barreling down the road, not wanting anyone or anything to get in our way. Let's be intentional about slowing down and taking in everything around us.

We often think of leading with empathy associated with listening, which is essential. However, empathy is further enhanced when we utilize our sight. Unfortunately, it's easy to blind ourselves to the needs of others by getting caught in a "Go, Go, Go" mentality, putting our heads down to move from one task to another and missing critical visual signs all around. We can't effectively lead others with empathy if we are operating at a hurried pace and not taking the time to slow down and use our eyes to look for the needs of others.

Hurry Sickness

So why do we speed through yellow lights? In our society today, we try to do too many things at one time, struggling to sit still. Our minds are constantly pulled, limiting our time in deep thought and deep relationships. We're always in a hurry. Instead, we spend most of our days switching our brains from surface-level thought to surface-level thought, with surface-level relationships limiting our connection with the people around us. We're antsy, jittery, and always ready to randomly touch a phone and scroll. Like an internet browser, our brains have so many tabs open at the top that we quickly shift back and forth between tabs, never being able to close one fully.

Before I know it, I have multiple browsers open with a growing number of tabs in each browser, and my mind can't grasp it all. Also, many of those tabs are action related because I've said yes to so many things that I'm constantly running back and forth between browsers and tabs (husband, father, coach, principal, church member, etc.). Do you know what happens to my computer when I have too many browsers and tabs open? The computer stops operating efficiently and effectively, and a loud fan comes on. The first thing I usually do is call the technology department to tell them my computer is functioning slowly and there's a loud noise coming from the laptop. It's as if I think they can save the day. Instead, I get the dreaded response that they say so kindly, "Did you try restarting your computer?" The last thing I want to do is restart my computer, even though I know that's what it needs. And after my computer restarts, I need to be intentional about not opening more browsers and tabs than the computer can handle. The same goes for us as leaders. We try to do too many things, significantly limiting our full potential. We often get so busy that we fail to see we need a "restart." When we operate this way, we miss our true calling as leaders: the people around us.

Dr. Caroline Leaf is a Christian Neuroscientist who uses the term "milkshake multitasking." Her research has found that one of the plagues of modern existence is multitasking, leading to hurry sickness and obsessive time management. Many of us live with a constant feeling of hurry, "needing" to get things done at all times. Dr. Leaf shares that the lack of quality in our thought lives and poor focusing of attention is the complete opposite of how our brains are designed to function. She notes, "Every rapid, incomplete, and poor quality shift of thought is like making a milkshake with your brain cells and neurochemicals" (Leaf, 2022). This is not how God designed our minds. Human beings are deeply intellectual beings made in God's image. As leaders, we must lead differently by slowing down and not trying to do it all. We may think we are "doing" a lot, but more than likely, we are missing out on leading the people around us and failing to empathize with their needs, wants, and desires.

I have found the days I am the "busiest" or "need to get things done" are when someone needs me the most. I'm confident I missed many moments connecting with my wife, my kids, a friend, or a coworker because I was in a hurry. Proverbs 12:25 tells us that "Anxiety weighs down the heart." Are you weighed down by trying to do too much? Trying to be too much? In a world and society that is moving faster and faster, slow down and look around to the needs of others. **Jesus was never in a hurry.**

Take Action

Empathy is enhanced when we slow down and use our time to show people we are happy to give them the time they need and deserve. Commit to slowing down. Leaders can be so "busy" that we often forget to pause and slow down. Literally, be cognizant of slowing down as you drive. If you typically drive in the left (fast) lane on the highway, drive in the right lane. Allow cars to whiz right by. As you drive slower, notice things around you becoming more clear. Praise God in traffic or when you get stopped at a red light. Praise God when something slows you down. What a great reminder for us that we are not in control - to slow down and come to a complete stop.

Purposefully walk slower in your homes and at work. Is there a family member, a spouse, or a child who needs you to stop into their room to ask how their day was or if everything is OK? Do you need to sit on the couch and talk with your spouse? Is there a co-worker or employee who needs you to stop by their office or classroom to check in and see how they're doing? Does someone in your life need your help? Quit being in such a hurry. Purposefully slow down—don't miss people by speeding right on by.

Empathize with Your "Glasses" On

When we slow down, we can see more clearly. I've worn contacts since I was in fifth grade. In fourth grade, I failed my eye exam at school–I couldn't even see the big letter E. Since I was so active in sports, my parents wanted me to skip glasses and go to contacts. I eventually got a pair of glasses I wear at night after taking my contacts out. Before going to bed, I place my glasses on my nightstand. Sometimes I hear the glasses fall to the floor as I don't put them entirely on the nightstand. Other times I knock the glasses over in the middle of the night when attempting to check the time.

My wife finds the next part of this story pretty funny. The mornings after I knock my glasses off my nightstand, I have to find my glasses on the floor. My vision is so poor that I must get on my hands and knees to find my glasses. I blindly rub and pat the carpet, hoping my hand bumps into the glasses - without them, I can't see. I don't know if you've ever been there before, but it's pretty challenging looking for glasses when you cannot see anything around you. During those times on my hands and knees, I can't see anything around me. My perspective is solely focused on me, my wants, and my needs. But yet, most times, I try to find the glasses myself when I can't see.

Now here's my wife's favorite part. While I'm on my hands and knees looking for my glasses, I'll often have to ask her to come over and help me. "Carly," I humbly whisper. "Can you come here quickly? My glasses fell off the nightstand, and I can't find them. I need your help. I can't see." She usually walks over and smiles at me with her 20/20 vision, locates the glasses immediately, and hands them to me. Once I have those glasses in my hands, I slide them onto my face, and I can see. My perspective completely changes–I can see everything around me.

How often do we, as leaders, get stuck in our leadership (like me, on the floor looking for my glasses) with tunnel vision, blind to the people and needs around us? How often do we fail to see the needs of others clearly as we go blindly through our to-do lists of what we need to accomplish? How often do we try to see on our own; when we really need to ask someone for help–someone to hand us a pair of glasses to help us see clearly? When we put our "glasses" on and change our perspective, we can see people differently. We can lead with empathy.

The moment I heard that testimony shared at our church, I immediately felt as if there was someone with me in my corner. If you take the analogy of a boxer, it previously had been like I was out in the ring fighting anxiety and depression day after day. When the round ended, I would return to my corner to prepare for the next round, but no one was there with me (or so I thought). Now it felt like someone was there, ready to help prepare, direct, and guide me through the next rounds. Before that, I thought I was alone, the only person going through such a struggle. I was wrong.

Remember how I had to ask my wife to hand me my glasses off the floor so I could see? That's what we need. We need people to help us see. We need them to hand us our "glasses." I was trying to see all by myself and missing everything around me. I needed help; I needed to ask for help. I began to open up to others, first with the people closest to me. I met with my wife and shared specific details of my struggle. I remember meeting with my parents on their back porch. I started to meet with my dad once a week. I met with my sisters and brothers-in-law to share the struggles I'd been hiding. My brother-in-laws are also my best friends. I shared some of my struggles with my principal at school, my 7th-grade team at the time, and an 8th-grade teacher down the hall. I called my pastor and spoke with him for about a half hour. I also did something I had been too embarrassed to do–I saw a counselor.

As I continued to open up with my struggles, my eyes and heart began (and continue) to be opened to the stories and struggles of people all around me–in my home and beyond. And the man who shared his testimony at church? He was the one who came over and helped me lay my foundation discussed in the opening chapter. It wasn't a one-time thing, as I've reached out to him many times over the past few years through life's inevitable ups and downs. He and others have walked beside me. Leading with empathy is handing each other a pair of glasses when we are on our hands and knees, unable to see. Sometimes you are the one giving others the glasses, helping them to see. Other times, you are the one needing the glasses. We need each other. Leading with empathy is leading with people.

Take Action

Not only do we need to ask God to open our eyes to the needs around us, we need to be intentionally intrusive in each other's lives to help us see clearly. Pray that God will guide you in contacting a close friend for help. Reaching out to others for help is never easy, but it's necessary. Is there a situation you're struggling to see clearly and need someone to hand you a pair of "glasses" by offering their perspective? It's okay admitting you can't do it alone, ask for help. You'll see better.

Empathize Through Questions

I noticed something unique about a school superintendent I worked with. He didn't ask basic questions like, "How are you?" or "How is your day?" When he saw me, he would ask, "What's your biggest challenge today?" Other times he would ask, "What's the most difficult thing you have to do this week?" He would ask a third question: "What's something coming up that has you feeling a little uncertain?" I began to notice a trend–those were empathetic questions designed to get beneath the surface of the traditional "How are you?" "I'm good," and move on with your day conversation. As an assistant principal then, I started to prepare for those questions when I saw him. I didn't always know how to answer them, especially at first, but they did cause me to pause and think. He often ended our conversations with, "What's something coming up that you're looking forward to?"

Not only did he ask the questions, but he also gave me his undivided attention as he listened to my response. I know he truly cared about what I had to say—those difficulties and challenges throughout a day or week. On top of that, he was always ready to follow my response up with a way he could help. His questions led to great conversation. Do you know why? He prioritized me and built a relationship with me. The relationship paved the way for me to open up to his empathetic questions and get beneath the surface level, allowing us to move into a genuine conversation as he listened and helped me grow.

Years later, about two weeks before the start of a new school year, I saw a teacher at the copy machine in the office. As I approached her, I was prepared to ask, "How are things going for you?" Instead, I heard the superintendent in the back of my mind asking me, "What's your biggest challenge right now?" After a quick hello, I saw the nerves and uncertainty in her eyes; she was a first-year teacher overwhelmed with the anticipation of what would come. I asked, "What's your biggest challenge as you approach your first school year?" As we stood at the copier, she responded with the uncertainty and stress paperwork was causing her (She was a special education teacher). We spoke for a few minutes, and I offered her support and reassurance but didn't think much of the conversation afterward. I closed the conversation with, "What's something coming up that you're looking forward to?" Her eyes lit up as she immediately spoke about connecting with her students and colleagues and getting to know the families.

I saw this new teacher at the district opening in-service two weeks later. She approached me and said, "Remember that day a couple of weeks ago when you saw me at the copy machine?" I nodded and said yes with a smile. She explained how much she needed to hear the question, "What's your biggest challenge as you approach your first school year?" Her eyes welled up with tears in the packed auditorium as she continued sharing how much she was struggling that day. She explained how reassuring it was to know that someone recognized that she was a new teacher two weeks before the start of a school year. She told me that if I had asked her, "How are things going?" she would have lied and said, "Good."

Internally I felt emotional as I listened to her speak, as I thought back to my superintendent, who asked me the same questions. She was right. Those empathetic questions meant more to me than I realized and opened up meaningful dialogue more than I realized. Empathizing with people is asking questions first, listening more, and speaking less. As James says, "Everyone should be quick to listen and slow to speak" (James 1:19). We can learn so much about people when we close our mouths and open our ears. Listening allows leaders to not only hear the words that are spoken, but understand why the words are being spoken.

Paul Tripp (2014) describes the importance of listening and asking questions beautifully:

Insightful people are not the people with the right answers, insightful people are the people with the right questions. Because you don't get to the right answers without the right questions— that's why Jesus taught by telling stories and asking questions.

Questions are one of the most effective ways to connect with others. We can better empathize with others when we listen more, speak less, and ask the right questions. Looking and listening allows leaders to build social awareness to diagnose and *learn* the needs of others and consider action steps to follow. We will look more closely at moving empathy into action in the next chapter. Leaders need to ask themselves where others are with an awareness to see through the lens of those they lead. Cognitive empathy, or "perspective-taking," is a process by which we observe others and "use our imagination and logic to discern what they must be thinking or feeling" (Sande, 2014). Like the question, "Where are they?" we want to constantly be looking and listening to *learn* what others need. Taylor (2022) states that we will *learn* to appreciate the emotions of others as a form of data helping us diagnose where people are, what they need, and what they don't. Too often, leaders move into action before taking the time to diagnose the needs around them. Leading with empathy requires adaptive leadership–adapting to the moment by looking and listening to *learn* to discern the needs of others.

Take Action

Seek to ask empathetic questions of others. Leaders often think we need to have the correct answers when we should focus on asking the right questions, listening, and learning to discern the needs of others. Skip over the basic questions like, "How are you?" or "How is your day going?" Remember, the truth is *rarely* told. The relationship you have with others will impact their responses to the questions. Try the following questions:

- What is the biggest challenge you're facing today?
- What is the most challenging thing you have to do this week?
- What is something coming up that you are looking forward?

You can follow those questions up with "How can I help?" or "What do you need from me?" It's easy to walk right by with a "How are you?" It takes effort to ask insightful, empathetic questions and listen intently to the response. Listen for ways that you can help or provide support. These questions help set the stage for compassion–observing the needs of others and moving into action.

Summary

As I mentioned earlier in the chapter, leadership doesn't mean we will *know* every person's story; it's recognizing every person *has* a story. Our days should be a mission to walk alongside others through their joys, celebrations, pain, and hurting, rejoicing with those who rejoice and

> Leadership doesn't mean we will *know* every person's story; it's recognizing every person *has* a story.

mourning with those who mourn (Romans 12:15). We are to carry the burdens for one another (Galatians 6:2).

When we lead with empathy, we show people we care. A culture of empathy deepens relationships, builds trust, and strengthens families, businesses, schools, and communities. A lack of empathy weakens relationships. As Teddy Roosevelt famously said, "Nobody cares how much you know until they know how much you care" (Roosevelt, n.d). Leadership is empathizing *with* people.

CHAPTER 4

Observe

Pillar #3 - Leadership is observing the needs
of others and responding with compassion.
"Each of you should look not only to your own interests,
but also to the interests of others."

Phillippians 2:4

One spring afternoon, I rode my bike around town with my three kids. We were having a great time, smiling and laughing as we cruised the streets. It was a beautiful day, and even though the kids were still relatively young, they could ride their own bikes. As we were riding, we got to a long gradual hill. I decided the best thing I could do was set an example for them and go out in front as the leader.

I went ahead of my three kids, showing them the way to the top of the hill. I began to peddle faster to help propel me toward the top of the hill. My legs were burning, but I kept going without looking back. I reached the top of the hill and rested under a stop sign while waiting for my kids to arrive any second. Unfortunately, as I looked back, I saw and heard a few things I was not expecting. Two of my children were halfway up the hill, standing beside their bikes. I heard my oldest daughter yell, "Dad, we can't do it!" My youngest was about a quarter of the way up the hill crying and yelling for me to come back down. "Daddy, come back!" I listened, but instead of going down the hill to meet them, I stayed at the top and waited for them to arrive as they walked their bikes.

Fast Forward a few weeks later, we were again out for a bike ride - enjoying our time together until we got near the hill. My oldest two started to say, "Let's find another way to go; we don't want to go to the hill. We can't do it." As we continued riding, I prepped them verbally. I said, "You can make it up the hill; I know you can!" I also added a little advice, "While we are approaching the hill, start to pedal faster so you can gain momentum to help you the whole way up the hill."

Off we went up the hill. Once again, I sped off towards the top of the hill to set the example. As I reached the top of the hill and stood under the stop sign, I turned around with no kids nearby. There they stood again off their bikes, a couple of kids crying, one even saying, "This isn't fun anymore. Let's just go home." We finished our bike ride that day with not everyone in the greatest of moods.

I began reflecting. I wanted the kids to get to the top of the hill. It wasn't about me getting to the top of the hill but my kids getting to the top. I recognized their moods had changed drastically over the past two bike rides. They were either crying or sharing their displeasure with the hill and how I was leading or failing to lead them, to be more exact, up the hill.

The following weekend, the kids and I headed out on our bikes. I was excited to face the hill when my middle daughter suggested, "Let's go a different way; I don't want to go to the hill." I listened, but no matter what, we were going to the hill that day. As we approached the hill, I spoke individually to all three. I rode my bike behind my oldest daughter and said, "You go ahead. You can do this; I will be right behind you." I pedaled my bike beside my two younger children and said, "You can do this. I'm going to be pedaling right here beside you."

As our legs burned, we moved closer and closer to the top of the hill. I saw my oldest daughter smiling at the top of the hill, as she exclaimed, "I made it!" I arrived at the top of the hill with the other two a few seconds later. That day we stood at the top of the hill for a few extra seconds, fist-bumping and high-fiving one another to celebrate everyone reaching the top.

A few days later, we headed out for another bike ride. Guess what they said this time? "Daddy, let's go to the hill!" I asked my daughter, "What helped you get to the top of the hill last time we rode?" Her response? "Because we knew you were right there with us." Wow. "*We knew you were right there with us.*" I had been trying to lead out in front, expecting them to follow and reach the top of the hill when all they needed was for me to observe their needs and respond with compassion by meeting each of them where they were. How often do we, as leaders, get out in front of those we lead and incorrectly assume they are right there with us and we're with them? It wasn't about me reaching the top of the hill but moving my three kids to the top. Leadership is not about the leader being out in front, reaching the "top" before anyone else. Leadership is about coming alongside the people we lead, observing their needs, meeting them where they are, and helping them reach their full potential–often heights they didn't think they could reach.

> Leadership is about coming alongside the people we lead, observing their needs, meeting them where they are, and helping them reach their full potential– often heights they didn't think they could reach.

Leadership is Compassionate

Another key finding in Gallup's research was that the most effective leaders understand their followers' needs (Rath and Conchie, 2008). The study found that one of the followers' four basic needs from their leader was *compassion* (we previously discussed *stability* and *trust*). This book is called Leading *with* PEOPLE and earlier in the book I shared the definition of *with* as: "accompanied by." The word *compassion* is derived from Latin roots "com" meaning "with, together" and "pati" meaning "to suffer." So, at its core, compassion can be understood as "to suffer with" (Compassion International, n.d.). People desire to know their leader cares about them as a person. When we take the vertical relationship with our Heavenly Father and spread it horizontally to the people we lead, we lead with a heart that *observes the needs of others and moves into action*. Make the time to be a student of all the people around you, prioritize them, genuinely get to know them, empathize, observe their needs, and move into action.

Leaders shouldn't stop at empathy but allow empathy to move us toward compassion. Empathizing should drive us to observe the needs of others and respond accordingly. We ought to respond to empathy with heartfelt compassion that moves us into action for the cause of another person. The actions we take have a far more significant impact than the words we speak.

> We ought to respond to empathy with heartfelt compassion that moves us into action for the cause of another person.

Observe and Respond Like the Good Samaritan

In the Parable of the Good Samaritan (Luke 10: 25-37), Jesus tells the crowd to "Love the Lord your God with all your heart and with all your soul and with all your strength and with all your mind and "Love your neighbor as yourself" (Luke 10:27). A man responded to Jesus asking, "and who is my neighbor?" (Luke 10:29). Jesus continues on and tells the story of a man traveling from Jerusalem to Jericho when he was attacked by robbers. They took his clothes, beat him, and left him half dead (Luke 10:30).

A priest was walking by, and when he saw the man, he moved to the other side of the road. A Levite came to the same place, saw the beaten man, and he, too, passed by on the other side of the road. As a Samaritan traveled, he "came to where the man was, and when he saw him, he took pity on him" (Luke 10:33). He went to the man and bandaged his wounds before putting him on his donkey to take him to an inn and care for him (Luke 10:34). The good Samaritan had compassion for the injured man.

Like the Priest and the Levite, many people choose to keep a safe distance from suffering and people who are hurting. How often do many of us move towards the "other side of the road" when there is an opportunity to help? Compassionate people are compelled to be God's hands and feet; they are obliged to act. Compassion is not simply empathizing with what someone is feeling or going through; compassion is recognizing the suffering and moving beyond empathy with a willingness to help (Compassion International, n.d.).

Compassion In Action

Compassion Is a Phone Call

I had just experienced another anxious trial in my life. It was mid-summer when I woke up in the middle of the night, drenched in sweat, heart pounding, nauseous, with an anxious mind. I hadn't experienced that feeling in years. For a few minutes, I thought, "Oh no, here we go again." Unlike years before when I kept everything to myself, the following day, I immediately talked to my wife and texted three people close to me who were walking alongside me on my journey to let them know I was struggling.

A short while later, one of the people I reached out to asked me to give them a call. As I spoke with my mentor, I shared all my concerns and uncertainty over the phone. It had been years since I felt that anxiousness, accompanied by all those physical symptoms again. One of my fears was that I would enter a season of feeling that way for an extended period of time as I had before. On the phone, my mentor began with a passage I had heard many times before. Proverbs 3:5-6:

> Trust in the Lord with all your heart and lean not on your own understanding. In all your ways acknowledge him and he will make your paths straight.

He asked, "Are you trusting God or your own strength?" Next, he painted the following picture for me. Picture Jesus holding us in the palm of his hands. He said that is where we are, and there is no safer place to be. It took me back to the children's song I would sing growing up, "He's got the whole world in his hands, He's got the whole world in his hands." He reminded me that God had me exactly where he wanted me to be. If I get a job, praise God. If I don't get a job, praise God. If things are going well, praise God. If things are not going so well, praise God. It's all in His hands; praise God, praise God. He reminded me not to look too far ahead and take it one day at a time, resting in God's goodness.

As my mentor came alongside me, he pointed out a few takeaways from Proverbs 3:5-6. First, trust in the Lord, not my own strength and understanding. He told me to give all my worries to God by acknowledging He is the Creator who has written all my days in His book before one of them came to be. He shared God's plan is perfect and that He will make my paths straight. Are you trusting God or relying on your strength as you lead? Picture Jesus holding you in the palm of His hands because that's precisely where you are. Trust in the Lord with all your heart and lean not on your own understanding.

Take Action

God's timing is perfect. Pray and ask God to open your eyes and heart to someone you can call as a "small" act of compassion. Show God's compassionate grace through genuine words to others. As you're on the phone, focus on being a listening ear for that person. The phone call may be all they need, or through the conversation, you'll discern additional ways they need your help.

Compassion Is Stacking Stones

Two months after that phone call, my friend invited me to breakfast to reflect on my most recent trial. He walked alongside me throughout the trial with compassion. It was a powerful breakfast. As we sat down together, he shared that after coming out of a trial, he likes to reflect with four steps. He encouraged me to do four things:

1. Name the trial. He challenged me to literally name that difficult season in my life.
2. Create a list of Bible passages and verses that guided me through the trial.

3. Reflect on how God brought me through the trial—how God saw me through it.
4. What did I learn about God during the trial, and what did I learn about me?

Through these four steps, he encouraged me to stack stones for every trial I faced to remember how God brought me through it—just like he did for Joshua and the Israelites. The people of Israel had crossed the Jordan River and entered the Promised Land. The Promised Land was not one great vacation; it was a place of battle and a place of trust. As the challenges grew for the Israelites, they knew they had to trust God through each trial.

God told Joshua to take twelve men from the people, one person from every tribe in Israel. God instructed them to take up 12 stones out of the Jordan River. Each tribe sent a representative to carry a large stone from the dry riverbed where Israel crossed over. The memorial's purpose was to show the generations to come about the great things God had done, the compassion He showed to the Israelites, and that His work would not be forgotten.

During our seasons of "drought," we must walk alongside each other, stacking stones, remembering the compassion God shows us and the great things He has done so we can show compassion to others. James Chapter 1 says, "Consider it pure joy, my brothers, when you face trials of many kinds because you know the testing of your faith develops perseverance. Perseverance must finish its work so you may be mature and complete, lacking nothing. Don't stack stones alone; stack stones together.

Take Action

Who do you know or who have you seen facing difficulties right now that you could help? We need to walk alongside each other, stacking stones, remembering the compassion God shows us and the great things He has done so we can show compassion to others. Choose to "stack stones" with someone. Arrange to spend time with them; it may be for coffee, breakfast, lunch, a workout, or something that works for the two of you. The person you need to stack stones with may be right there in your house. Whichever route you choose, focus on these four questions:

1. Name the trial - literally name the difficult season in your life.
2. Create a list of Bible passages and verses that guided you through the trial.
3. Reflect on how God brought you through the trial—how God saw you through it.
4. What did you learn about God during the trial, and what did you learn about yourself?

Compassion is Dropping What You're Doing

A few years ago, my family was headed to Ocean City, New Jersey, for a week-long vacation over the 4th of July holiday. Our vehicle was packed as can be, including three excited kids on the inside and a bike rack carrying five bikes on the outside. I took a picture before we left because our car looked so comical, weighed down by luggage and people on the inside and five bikes on the back.

We started our vacation music playlist and headed down the road. I felt a little nervous about the bikes, so about two minutes from home,

I got out of the car to check on them. My professional inspection gave the bike rack a good shake, deemed it safe, and then returned to the car for the remaining two hour and fifteen-minute drive to Ocean City. I confidently told my wife "We are good to go." Only about three minutes later, I heard a loud thud. As I glanced in the rearview mirror, I saw my six-year-old daughters' bike rolling down the street. The remaining four bikes were dragging on the road behind the car.

I think it's only right that I share a little history on the bike rack. My wife bought it used off Facebook Marketplace. She's always looking to save a little bit of money. We later learned that the bike rack must have broken at one point for its previous owner and was put back together with a poor welding job. But hey, I'm not here to blame my wife (even though I thought we should buy a brand new one!). The used bike rack couldn't carry the weight of the bikes and snapped. Thankfully no one was injured, and only one bike was not rideable.

However, now we were stuck on the side of the road. We had all these bikes and a broken bike rack with no room inside the car. We called my brother-in-law, who was at the scene with two of his daughters in no time, ready to help. We planned to see if he could help us return the bikes to our house - we were going to turn around and leave our bikes at home. Here's the thing: not only did he help remove our broken bike rack and trash it for us, but he selflessly removed the bike rack from his car and put it onto ours. He helped us load our bikes again, and we continued to the shore. Some of our best memories of that trip to Ocean City, New Jersey, were the family bike rides on the boardwalk and through the alleyways around town. They wouldn't have been possible without my brother-in-law's help and compassion.

My brother-in-law's actions were a great example of compassionate leadership. He immediately stopped what he was doing and gave us a hand on the side of the road. Not only did he help us out, but he also took his bike rack and put it in our car for our family to enjoy on our vacation. That's leadership. Leadership is stopping what you're doing and helping someone in need. Leadership is selflessly giving your time and resources to ensure someone has what they need—even if it inconveniences you. Much like my family's bike rack incident, sometimes all it takes is one person to come alongside with compassion, giving you a hand, lending some encouragement, and sending you back out on your way—often at the just the right moment.

Take Action

Ask God to prepare your heart and open your eyes to the immediate needs around you. Be intentional about stopping whatever you are doing to help someone in need. You can show God's compassion to others through unexpected gestures of kindness. It may be someone you don't even know. Keep your heart and eyes open.

Compassion Is a "Hug"

In August of 2022, a scary scene occurred in the Little League World Series Regional Tournament in Waco, Texas. Every year 11 and 12-year-old baseball players from all across the country and world dream of advancing to play at the Little League World Series held in Williamsport, Pennsylvania. These games are even played on ESPN. To earn a trip to Williamsport in August, teams must win and advance through many tournaments. The last tournament between the players and the Little League World Series is their regional tournament. These games are passion-filled with smiles, sweat, and tears as these 11 and 12-year-olds give it their all.

In the Southwest Regional Final, a player named Isaiah Jarvis from Tulsa, Oklahoma, was batting against Kaiden Shelton, the pitcher for Pearland, Texas. Shelton lost control of one of his pitches, and it drilled

Jarvis in the helmet. The impact of the fastball caused Jarvis' helmet to fly off his head as he dropped to the ground. Jarvis received medical attention and was cleared to go to first base after the hit by pitch.

As Jarvis stood on first base, he could see the pitcher was visibly distraught, in tears on the mound, after hitting him in the head with a pitch. Kaiden was struggling to compose himself to continue pitching. What happened next was a powerful, humbling scene. Unprompted and on his own, Jarvis removed his helmet at first base, threw it on the ground, and walked directly to the pitcher's mound. When arriving at the pitcher's mound, Jarvis wrapped his arms around Kaiden and hugged him for nearly twenty seconds, sharing a few words. "Hey, you're doing great," Jarvis could be heard saying to Kaiden on the mound.

That day's scene was such a powerful example of empathy moved to compassion. After the game, Jarvis said, "I just wanted to go over there and make sure he was all right. Make sure he knows that I'm all right. And really just encourage him." This example from these Little Leaguers is something we can take into our homes, our workplaces, or wherever we're leading. Sometimes we need to stop what we're doing, "throw our helmets" to the side and go let someone know they're doing great. Compassion doesn't have to be a grand gesture; it can be a literal or metaphorical hug. It only takes a minute to pause and let someone around us know we see them, we empathize with them, and we're there for them. We often find ourselves on both sides of the scene. Some days we are Kaiden struggling to continue in a "game," and we need someone to come out and encourage us. Other times we are Jarvis: we see someone struggling

> It only takes a minute to pause and let someone around us know we see them, we empathize with them, and we're there for them.

around us and are moved to compassion by offering encouraging words or gestures to let them know it will be OK.

When I think back to the time when anxiety struck and I passed out at work, I picture the people who immediately showed simple acts of compassion. There was a group of people circled around to ensure I was OK. At the time, I didn't realize the powerful impact that scene would have on the rest of my life and leadership—the recognition and importance of needing to be surrounded by people throughout life. Two people walked by my side from the classroom to the nurse's office to make sure I was fine every step of the way. My brother-in-law drove me home, and when I arrived home, my wife met me with a hug in the middle of the kitchen. All these acts were examples of compassion: walking alongside one another, letting people know it's going to be all right, and that we're in this together.

Take Action

Ask God to make you more aware of situations where you could come alongside others with comfort and support. Choose to pause and reflect on who needs to know that "you are right there with them." Don't incorrectly assume that the people you lead are right there with you, and that you're right there with them. Are you trying to lead out in front, expecting others to follow when what they need is for you to slow down, observe their needs, and respond with compassion? Come alongside people and meet them "where they are." Remember, compassion doesn't have to be a grand gesture; it can be a literal or metaphorical hug. It only takes a minute to pause and let someone around us know we see them, we empathize with them, and we're here for them.

Compassion Is Taking a Leap of Faith

Jonathan Alsheimer is a best-selling author and internationally known keynote speaker. He is a teacher who is passionate about what he does. But most importantly, Jonathan is compassionate, and his compassion shines through in all he does. Jonathan and his students are good Samaritans. Jonathan covers American History in his classroom, specifically the rise of industrialization in America. During the industrialization unit, he has students work in groups to create their own businesses each year. After a challenging personal situation with his daughter, Jonathan decided to change things up and collaborate with his students to build a non-profit from the ground up.

A few years earlier, one of Jonathan's precious daughters was hospitalized for surgery. After the surgery, she was in so much pain she couldn't speak. You can imagine how hard it must have been for the Alsheimer family to see their daughter in that much pain and discomfort. One night a nurse walked into the hospital room with a box and handed the box to Jonathan's daughter. The box was filled with fun little items for kids. One item that stood out above the rest for Jonathan's daughter was a stuffed unicorn that she held tight throughout her hospital visit. The box completely lifted her spirits and the spirits of her family. She smiled as she looked through the box and held the unicorn tightly.

That's when Jonathan got an idea that moved from empathy to compassion. He returned to his classroom and talked to his students about an opportunity to make a difference in the lives of kids by starting a non-profit. The non-profit would raise money to collect items for kids in hospitals experiencing difficult situations. That is when the nonprofit *From Kids to Kids* was born. The nonprofit's name, *From Kids to Kids*, has subsequently been changed to *A Rae of Hope* in honor of Jonathan's mother, a teacher who passed away from cancer.

A Rae of Hope is a student-led program focusing on compassion to help bring smiles to kids and their families in the hospital. When the students began collaborating with Mr. Alsheimer on this project, they were all in. One student shared, *"What we're doing is going to impact lives and bring a smile to their faces, even when they are going through hard things."* The students began to raise money and search for stuffed animals, pop its, crayons, coloring books, and more to fill boxes and send to kids in the hospital facing difficulties. Another student shared how the efforts with the nonprofit showed her how she can think about others and make a difference in their lives. Jonathan reminds the class and other educators that we do not just teach content; we teach character, and our actions will speak louder than our words. As Jonathan's late grandmother-in-law, Shirley Chapman, always said, "Share the good news often and when necessary, use words." That's powerful.

> We do not just teach content; we teach character, and our actions will speak louder than our words.

Jonathan could have stopped at empathy, understanding, and sharing the feelings of kids and families struggling in the hospital, but he didn't; he moved into action. Jonathan often says, "Titles don't make leaders. Actions do." That's compassion: observing the needs of others and moving into action. Not only did he move into action, but he also moved a classroom of seventh-grade students into action. How cool is that? Stop and think for a minute about the life lesson and domino effect this nonprofit, *A Rae of Hope*, will have on his students' lives and the impact they will continue to have on others throughout their lifetime. *A Rae of Hope* was seen across social media and news outlets, leading others to reach out about doing this in their classrooms and schools, causing the project to grow throughout the nation. Most importantly, think about the effect moving from empathy into action will have on those kids sitting in the hospital rooms and the smiles these boxes are and will continue to bring to their faces.

Take Action

Choose to take a step of faith. Begin in prayer, asking God to strengthen you with His wisdom, guidance, and discernment. Is there something that's been on your heart that you're ready to take action on? It could be an idea for starting a nonprofit organization, going on a mission trip, organizing a fundraiser event, or traveling a long distance to see a friend or family member you haven't seen in a while. Is there a broken relationship in your life in which you can show God's grace and compassion? Be bold and courageous—take a step of faith.

Summary

Like the Good Samaritan, as leaders, we need to move beyond empathy and lead with compassion. Leading with compassion doesn't mean we need to start a nonprofit organization, but if something like that is on your heart, go for it. *Leading with compassion means individuals know we see them, we see their needs, and we care*—it's making a difference one life at a time. Leadership isn't for show; it's walking humbly and quietly alongside others through life's "little" moments.

Remember my daughter's response in the opening story of what helped her bike to the top of the hill? *"We knew you were right there with us."* Let's not be leaders like the Priest and the Levite who crossed over to the other side of the road when they saw a person in need; let's be like the Good Samaritan who observed a need, acted, and was right there with the man who was injured, beaten, and robbed. Have compassion on one another because of God's undeserved, unfailing compassion for us. People need to know we are right there with them. That's compassion; that's leadership. Leadership is observing the needs of others and responding with compassion.

> People need to know we are right there with them. That's compassion; that's leadership.

CHAPTER 5

Pray

Pillar #4 - Leadership is *praying* for and with people.
"Pray continually."

1 Thessalonians 5:17

While serving as an assistant principal, I sat with my building principal when I noticed a black notebook near his desk. I saw the notebook over the next few weeks but didn't think much of it. I saw him writing in the notebook as I passed his office a few weeks later. As the weeks continued on, I noticed a trend. I would see him engaging in what looked to be a serious conversation, and then he would write in the black notebook.

We were scheduled to meet to prepare for an upcoming faculty meeting, so I arrived and sat in his office. I saw him conversing with a teacher through the glass in the hallway before returning to his office. The conversation looked relatively serious, and I saw tears in the teachers' eyes. As the principal returned, I noticed he first took out his black notebook. I said to him, "Can I ask you something?"

He said, "Of course, go ahead."

I said, "I've noticed that black notebook beside your desk; what's it for?"

He smiled gently, held the black notebook in his hand, and said, "Every leader needs a little black notebook."

We never met about the faculty meeting that day. Instead, he told me all about how he uses the black notebook. He shared that the notebook was used to write down all of the personal things people were going through that they shared with him. As he navigated many conversations with teachers, support staff, families, and students, he would add those difficult situations to his little black notebook. He would use the notebook to follow up and check in on how people were doing and, more importantly, use it as a prayer book for the people he led.

The principal would keep that notebook by his desk at school, put it in his bag to go home, and utilize it as a prayer list. One line he shared with me stuck out more than others: *"They may never see me praying for them, their situation, or family, but it is the most powerful thing I can do for them and our school."*

Pray Like David

David is one of my favorite people in the Bible. Yes, the shepherd boy defeated Goliath with a stone, became King of Israel, and committed a great sin. But David feared the Lord; he was repentant and faithful in prayer no matter the circumstances. He poured out his heart to God for guidance, wisdom, and discernment. David knew that God's thoughts were higher than his, God's ways were bigger than his, and God could do so much more than he could do on his own. David was a man after God's own heart, and nine times in the books of 1st and 2nd Samuel, David *inquired of the Lord*. David's practice of faithfully inquiring of the Lord no matter his circumstances is a beautiful prayer model we can utilize in our lives. When you feel your worries and anxieties rise, pause and turn those worries into prayers inquiring about wisdom and discernment from the Lord.

If you're unsure of where to start in the Bible, the book of Psalms is the perfect place. Many psalms were read or sung as part of worship, demonstrating that God is worthy of our praise, regardless of our circumstances. Are you feeling sorrowful? How about anger or frustration? Fear, regret, stress, anxiety? What about joy? You will find it all in the Psalms. They are relatable no matter how you are feeling or your current situation, and, most importantly, they point to our Heavenly Father. The Psalms exemplify how we can pray, honestly pouring our hearts out to God.

Leadership is Praying Over Everything

A mentor once told me, "Pray over everything." He shared how he views his business as "God's business," turning everything over to God in prayer. Leadership is heavy and filled with family, friends, colleagues, and employees going through extreme challenges and awesome celebrations. Paul says in Timothy 1:2, "I urge, then, first of all, that petitions, prayers, intercession, and thanksgiving be made for all people." Intercessions are requests we make to God on behalf of others, and the needs of others should have a place in our daily prayers. Paul's words exemplify the importance of prioritizing our prayers for all people. When we take the vertical relationship with our Heavenly Father and spread it horizontally to the people we lead, we lead with a heart that *prays* for people.

<u>Praying for All People Means...</u>
Pray for your spouse.
Pray for your kids.
Pray for family and friends.

Pray for those you get along with.
Pray for those you struggle to get along with.
Pray for those who are kind to you.
Pray for those who are unkind to you.
Pray for those who agree with you.
Pray for those who disagree with you.
...pray for them by name.
Pray for wisdom, guidance, and discernment.
Pray for strength....
....and the list can go on.

Where Can We Pray?

Pray in your room.
Pray in your home.
Pray as you exercise.
Pray in your car.
Pray as you walk into work.
Pray as you walk through the hallways.
Pray in your office.
Pray as you mow the lawn.
Pray as you wash the dishes.
Pray wherever you are...

When Can We Pray?

Pray when you rise in the morning.
Pray throughout your day.
Pray as you lay your head on your pillow at night.
Pray when you can't sleep.
Pray when things are going well.
Pray when things aren't going well.
Pray continually (1 Thessalonians 5:17).

Pause and Take a Deep Breath

Where does prayer rank on your daily list of priorities?

Waymaker

My wife and I were shopping one morning when she thought she would be funny and pointed to a sign, laughed, and said, "Hey, that reminds me of you." The sign read:

> Even when I don't see it, You're working
> Even when I don't feel it, You're working
> You never stop, You never stop working

My wife knew those were song lyrics, but she wanted to get in a little dig about how much I had been working. I smiled (she wasn't wrong), but it did cause me to pause and think of the goodness of God and the significance of prayer. The song is called "Waymaker" (Sinach 2015) and focuses directly on God, who He is, and what He is doing. Several Christian artists, such as Michael W. Smith, Mandisa, Leeland, and Passion, have covered the song. A waymaker makes a way and that is exactly who God is—He doesn't just make *a* way; He makes *the* way. We won't always see or feel when God's working, but we can pray continually to God, resting in the truth that He never stops working for our good. As Romans 8:28 says, "And we know that in all things God works for the good of those who love him, who have been called according to his purpose. Although we and the people around us face sufferings at this present time" (Romans 8:18), God is working for our good and His good. He is not working some things for our good, but *all* things. That doesn't mean things will be easy. But God's help is an enduring promise as we are called to pray without ceasing. He is the Waymaker.

Pause and Take a Deep Breath

As my mentor shared, pray over everything. God is our compass. He guides us where we need to go and directs us in what we need to do. God will always point us in the right direction. He's the One who has the whole world in his hands. You have a direct, 24-hour-a-day, 7-days-a-week line of communication with the Creator of this world. God is the waymaker who not only points you in the right direction, but comes along with you every step of the way. Your guide is the One who created the entire map. Too often, we think we need to figure things out on our own when we can pray to God and trust that He is leading us in the right direction.

Prayer in Action

Pray to God, Your Helper

Prayer is surrender; it humbly points us to God, recognizing apart from Him, we can do nothing. As leaders, our lives are filled with many people, opportunities, and responsibilities. I was walking one morning and knew I needed help. I felt overwhelmed and was at a spot where I didn't know what to pray or whom to pray for. Have you ever been there? You know you need help, you know you need to pray, but you can't find the words, what to say, or who to pray for. David says in Psalm 62:8, "Trust in him at all times, O people; pour out your hearts to him, for God is our refuge."

I began to pour out my heart to God. Psalm 121:1 says, "I lift my eyes to the hills—where does my help come from? My help comes from the Lord, the Maker of Heaven and Earth." There's only one place to go when we don't know where to go. I began to pray, "*God help me.*"

<u>God help me as a husband</u> - Be my strength to lift Carly up today. What does *she* need today? I can't do it on my own, and I need you. Help me to see how I can best meet her needs and care for her. I trust that you will intercede and care for me, Lord. Lift her up as a wife, and a mother, in her work, and all her daily tasks. Help direct me on how to pray for her. Help me love her as Christ loved the church and gave himself up for her. I know I don't have the strength on my own; be my helper, be my strength.

<u>God, help me as a father</u> - Give me the strength I need, Lord; fill me with your daily bread. I need to remember to take it one day at a time. Build me up as a father, Lord. Help me to be present with Olivia, Isaac, and Eliot, looking out for their interests, not my own. I pray for each of them, Lord. I pray for their minds, bodies, and, most of all, their hearts. I pray that they would know and love you. Help me to encourage, guide, and build them up. What do they need today? Intercede for me and be my helper.

<u>God, help me as a principal</u> - There are so many people and so many needs, Lord. Help strengthen and show me how to best serve and care for others. Fill me with your wisdom and discernment as I navigate decisions. Open my eyes to the needs around me and how I can best serve and lead. There are far too many burdens for me to carry on my own; I give them to you, God. Be my helper.

<u>God, help me in all my relationships</u> - I don't want to miss the needs around me. Help me be like Jesus, serving those around me and pointing them to you. I don't want it to be about me, but all too often, that's what I quickly allow it to become: all about me. I need you and can't do

it alone. Open my eyes, Lord. Open my eyes and heart to the people in my life and what they need. Be my helper.

Take Action

Pour out your heart to God in prayer and cry out to Him. Don't let your finite mind limit the Almighty God. Ask God to be your helper in each leadership role you serve. What blanks can you fill in?

God, help me as a _____.

What various roles do you serve that you need to hand over to God? Maybe you don't even know where to start. If so, try praying, *"God, I lift my eyes to you. I don't know what or who to pray for, but my help comes from you, the One who made the heavens and the earth. Show me the needs around me; open my eyes, Lord. Be my helper."*
Remember, God doesn't desire the perfect prayer; He desires your heart. Pour out your heart to God and watch Him work.

Pray for Others

Every Labor Day weekend, my family gathers with our longtime family friends at a campfire. It is the Sunday evening before Labor Day when we gather around the campfire for prayer, praise, and worship. What is so encouraging about this group around the campfire is that they were formed many years ago through my parent's Bible study. The relationships and friendships have passed down from generation to generation. You can find grandparents, parents, and many kids as we gather.

What is most special about this time of prayer around the campfire is that we are doing life together, walking alongside one another through the good and the bad, the ups and the downs. We share praises and how we've seen God work over the past year since we last gathered by the campfire. We also share needs, struggles, and hardships. After sharing, we go around the campfire praying prayers of praise, thanksgiving, and petition for one another. That's not always easy, but it started with the deep relationships that everyone formed with one another—a relationship in which trust was built to open up to one another.

The prayer time is an encouraging, uplifting time to pray with one another, carrying each other's burdens and standing in the gap for one another. *Not only do we pray for one another that night, we take those prayers into our homes and continue praying for one another.* There's just something uplifting about praying to God with others, lifting each other up in prayer.

Take Action

Commit to praying for others throughout the day. We are called to be devoted to prayer, watchful, and thankful (Colossians 4:2). Prayer is not meant to be an event only performed at certain times, but prayer is an ongoing dialogue with the Lord. As you walk through your day, praise God for the people in your life. Pray for the people inside your home, pray for friends and family, and pray for others throughout your day. Pray continually (1 Thessalonians 5:17).

Commit to keeping a prayer notebook. When we get to know the people we lead, we learn their stories, and we can respond with compassion. We can then lift those people up in prayer. Find a book or journal to keep a list of the needs, struggles, and celebrations of the people in your life. The book will be a valuable resource to guide your prayer life.

Pray with Others

I was attending a Pennsylvania principal conference when I met Tyler Cook, a principal from Erie, Pennsylvania. Conferences are always an excellent opportunity to meet people and build your network. After I finished presenting a session, Tyler and I decided to meet in the hotel lobby for coffee. As we sat in the middle of the hotel lobby, people passed by one after another. Tyler and I spoke about our passion for leadership, our faith in Jesus, and our families. We talked for over an hour when it was time to head to our next sessions. Before we got up from the table, we prayed together. I'll never forget that moment; the busy hotel lobby became still as we bowed our heads and closed our eyes. In the midst of many, we went to the Lord in prayer. I can still feel the encouragement from Tyler's prayer–thanking God that our paths crossed, strengthening me as a leader in my various roles as husband, father, and principal.

Here's the thing, though: Tyler didn't know this, but I was struggling at that time. I needed that conversation, that prayer, at that exact moment. We don't just want to pray *for* each other; we want to pray *with* each other, building each other up and encouraging one another. Through his prayer, Tyler helped carry my burdens for me (Galatians 6:2). As Jesus said, where two or three come together in my name, there I am with them (Matthew 18:20). When Tyler and I prayed for one another, it surrendered my "me-centered" thoughts and focused me on going to Almighty God to lift Tyler up. Prayer brings us closer to God and closer to one another. When we pray, we humble ourselves by focusing on God and His will for our lives. Prayer allows us to become more aware of the people and needs around us, strengthening our relationship with God and others.

Take Action

We can't do it alone; we are made to be in community. Pray that God would place a prayer partner on your heart, someone you can navigate life with through prayer on a consistent basis. Maybe you already have one. How could having a prayer partner enhance your prayer life and daily walk? We can encourage and support each other as we pray for each other's needs and turn every blessing back into praise. Jesus tells us in Matthew 18:20, "For where two or three come together in my name, there I am with them." Carry each other's burdens and stand in the gap for one another as you boldly go out in God's confidence. Remember, Jesus sent his disciples out 2 x 2. Don't go through life alone.

Pray with Your Ears

Our family loves driving around and listening to praise and worship songs. One of our favorite songs is "Build a Boat" by Colton Dixon (2023). The song tells the story of Noah's faithfulness to God in building the ark. Dixon was inspired to write the song after revisiting the story of Noah in the Bible and how God asked Noah to start building the ark while in the middle of a drought before there was any rain. Here's the chorus:

> I will build a boat in the sand where they say it never rains
> I will stand up in faith, I'll do whatever it takes
> With your wind in my sails, your love never fails or fades
> I'll build a boat so let it rain
> And when the flood and water start to rise, yeah
> I'll ride the storm cause I got you by my side

With your wind in my sails, your love never fails or fades
I'll build a boat so let it rain

The next three lines following the chorus go on to say:

You're the map, You're my compass
You help me navigate the currents underneath
Take the lead, I surrender

That's what prayer is - surrendering to God and giving him the lead. I'll admit I like to be in control. I'll also be the first to admit I'm not in control of anything. Read what Noah did as God was directing him to build the ark:

Genesis 6:22 - Noah did everything just as the Lord commanded him.
Genesis 7:5 - And Noah did all that the Lord commanded him.
Genesis 6:9 - He walked faithfully with God.

You've probably found I'm a fan of fill-in-the-blanks, so let's pause and complete a few. Reflect honestly. Can you fill in your name in the blanks below?

_____ did everything just as the Lord commanded.
And _____ did all that the Lord commanded.
_____ walked faithfully with God.

Noah filled his name in all three, and that's powerful. We often think of prayer as talking to God. While that's a significant part of prayer, like Noah, we must listen to God. It's hard to sit still, be quiet and listen. In those quiet moments, we can walk with God every step of the way—listening, being filled with knowledge, wisdom, and discernment about what we should do or shouldn't do next for ourselves, our families, and all those we lead. We have become all too accustomed to instant responses—emails, text messages, social media—it's at our fingertips. We thrive off the next notification to get our answer and move on. Think of Amazon: one click, and we have something shipped to us the next day. My family lives in Pennsylvania, and we were on vacation in Florida when my wife needed to order something for the plane ride home. She went into Amazon, changed the delivery address, placed the order, and boom; the package found its way to our doorstep in Florida.

That's often how we treat our prayer life. We want immediate answers from God (and typically the answer *we* desire). How often do we pause, stop, and listen to what God is telling us or has already told us? Like Noah, we ought to respond in obedience through listening. Don't let your earthly "immediate" needs and desires get in the way of God's greater plan for you and the people you lead.

Take Action

Are you taking—or should I say making—the time to be still and *listen* to God? Be still and know that He is God, the Creator of this world, and you are not. Trust Him to be everything you need to be as you listen to where God wants you to move into action. Sometimes (oftentimes), listening requires waiting and patience. You'll be amazed at how much God is working in your waiting. Listen and trust Him.

Turn Your Worry List Into a Prayer List

The combination of personal needs and daily stresses has the potential to debilitate leaders with anxiousness and worry. In Philippians 4:6, Paul tells us what to do instead of worrying and tells us to turn everything over to God in prayer. Yes, *everything*.

Early one morning, a principal friend of mine was so overwhelmed with worries that he sat at his dining room table and began writing. He couldn't sleep the night before as he lay awake thinking about a few students, staff members, and families. One staff member had to leave school the day before because her daughter struggled with mental health needs. Another staff member was going to be out for a few weeks due to a sports injury to her child's head, and at that point, they were not sure what the outcome would be. Over the weekend, he learned that a student's father had passed away and a staff member had lost her mother.

Additionally, it was a challenging school year; the stresses of the Covid-19 pandemic were high, and every day was filled with teacher and support staff shortages, along with a few extreme student behavioral needs throughout the day. The news recently was filled with a senseless school tragedy. And lastly, he is a husband and father carrying the weight of meeting his family's needs.

He began by putting the word "worry" at the top of a notebook paper and started writing. He poured everything he worried about onto the page – the list grew. As he wrote, he reflected on all the people going through difficult situations and his worries at school and home. After completing his list, he returned to the top of the paper and crossed out the word "Worry." He replaced the word "Worry" with "Prayer." The principal went back through every item one by one in prayer. As Paul said in Philippians, we must pray and petition to God about everything, not worry. Everything on that list was important to God. There's nothing too big or too small to talk to God about. He cares about every detail of our lives and the lives of those all around us.

God already knows our requests before we pray them, yet He desires us to pray to Him with supplication, directly asking Him to do something. We are not called to pray before God with whining and complaining. We are to do all things without complaining or arguing

(Philippians 2:14) and go to God with thanksgiving (1 Thessalonians 5:18). Harry Ironside (n.d.) said, "We would worry less if we praised more. Thanksgiving is the enemy of discontentment and dissatisfaction." We have such an opportunity in leadership, surrounded by so many people and responsibilities, to take everything to God in prayer for strength, wisdom, and discernment.

Take Action

Choose to turn all your worries into prayer. Be intentional about memorizing Philippians 4:6: *"Do not be anxious about anything, but in everything, by prayer and petition, with thanksgiving, present your requests to God."*

As you feel your anxiousness or worry on the rise, do the following:

1. Pause and acknowledge your worries, fears, and uncertainties.
2. Write "Worry List" at the top of a paper or journal page.
3. List everything overwhelming you with worry.
4. Return to the top of the paper and cross out the word "Worry."
5. Recite Philippians 4:6 - *"Do not be anxious about anything, but in everything, by prayer and petition, with thanksgiving, present your requests to God."*
6. Replace the word "Worry" with "Prayer."
7. Turn the worry list over to God in prayer.
8. Over the next week, month, or beyond, look back over the prayer list - what do you notice?

Summary

As my principal said, "*They may never see me praying for them, their situation, or their family, but it is the most powerful thing I can do for them.*" We could have so much to worry about in our leadership roles, but most importantly, we have much to pray about. Paul says in Philippians 4:7, "And the peace of God, which transcends all understanding, will guard your hearts and your minds in Christ Jesus. We ought to turn those late nights and early mornings from times of worry to times of prayer. The mind is a powerful thing. Who of you by worrying can add a single hour to his life (Matthew 6:27)? Instead, pray continually for others (1 Thessalonians 5:17) and allow the peace of God to transcend your earthly understanding guarding your heart and mind. We're not in control; go to the One who is and let Him be your guide. One of the most impactful ways to lead people is by what they may never see: Prayer. Leadership is praying for and with people.

CHAPTER 6

Love

Pillar #5 - Leadership is loving people.
Do everything in love.

1 Corinthians 16:14

"But I trust in your unfailing love." As I struggled through my season of anxiety and depression, I repeated these seven words over and over from Psalm 13. The entire Psalm from David hit close to home for me in describing how I was feeling:

> How long, O Lord? Will you forget me forever?
> How long will you hide your face from me?
> How long must I wrestle with my thoughts and every day have
>   sorrow in my heart?
> How long will my enemy triumph over me?

David asks God four times, "How long?" That's how I felt. How long will this depression last? How long will I feel this way? God, I'm trying hard; how long will you forget about me? How long will this anxiety and depression triumph over me? I was defeated and desired this great anguish to go away. Of course, God did not forget about me, but it felt that way.

Like my three young kids in the car, "Dad, how long until we are there?" A few minutes later, "Dad, how much longer now?" They grow increasingly restless and troubled in the back seat, tired of sitting so close to their siblings, wondering how long until they reach their destination and can get out of the car. Do you know what I have found helps them during these times of waiting? When I put the GPS on, they can see how much longer the trip will be and when we will arrive. They also love watching the screen to see every turn we need to make to reach our destination.

Oh, how that image of my kids in the car is a picture of my restless heart. It's as if during my trial, I wanted God to put on a GPS and show me how many more minutes were left in my pain. I wanted God to show me my arrival time. When will it end? How long, how long, how long, how long?

In verse three, David cries out to the Lord, "Look on me and answer, O Lord my God." Again, the same can be said for my kids in the car. They cry out, often literally, "Answer me, Dad! Help me see how many more minutes, help me to know when we will get there, and this will all be over. When will this end?"

Guess what I tell my kids in the car? "*It's all going to be OK. You don't have to worry about it. Daddy is driving and will get us there. We will be there before you know it. It's all going to be okay. Trust me. I love you.*"

Much like that typical scene in the car with my kids, my desire for God to take my pain away turned to impatience. The impatience led and often leads me to wrestle with my own thoughts (v.2). Looking inside myself and wrestling with my thoughts only breeds more anguish and despair in my heart. We are to take every thought captive and make it obedient to Christ (2 Corinthians 10:5). I didn't see reality and cried out to God to open my eyes. As we saw in the last chapter on prayer, we always need to cry out to God to open our eyes.

By God's grace and mercy, I kept returning to the first seven words of Psalm 13:5, "But I trust in your unfailing love." The Psalm concludes with, "My heart rejoices with your salvation. I will sing to the Lord for he has been good to me" (v. 5-6). David began to direct his feelings to the One who could do something about them instead of allowing his emotions to control him. He trusted in God's unfailing love knowing he could only find deep-rooted joy in God's love for him.

Love Like Jesus

There's a local cafe and grill fifteen minutes from my house named Agape. The restaurant's name comes from the ancient Greek word often used to describe Christ's love for people. Agape is not a feeling or emotion, not subjective to any conditions; it is unconditional, sacrificial love. Agape love is selfless, striving for the greatest good of others. It's love that can only come from God. We are called to love one another (1 John 3:11). The love of Christ ought to drive us to love others.

1 John 3:16-20
This is how we know what love is: Jesus Christ laid down his life for us. And we ought to lay down our lives for our brothers. If anyone has material possessions and sees his brother in need but has no pity on him, how can the love of God be in him? Dear children, let us not love with words or tongue but with actions and truth."

Pause and Take a Deep Breath

God is love, and only through God can we show unfailing, unconditional love to the people we lead. We have a choice to make, and the choice we need to make as a leader is to strive for the good of others. Agape love is unconcerned with self and concerned with the greatest good of one another.

Leading with Love

When I was preparing to take a new job as a school principal, the outgoing principal unexpectedly gave me the best leadership advice I have ever received: "The moment I could stop trying to be the 'perfect principal' and just focus on showing Christ's love...it all came together." No job in leadership is more important than showing Christ's love to others. When we take the vertical relationship with our Heavenly Father and spread it horizontally to the people we lead, we lead with a heart that *loves* people. Great leaders love people; it only takes one relationship to help someone feel like they belong and are loved.

> No job in leadership is more important than showing Christ's love to others.

Author Ann Voskamp said, "No matter what happens in the world, the truth is always this: you were formed by Love for love" (Voskamp, 2014). But what does loving others look like? There's no better place to break down what love is than 1 Corinthians 13 verses 4-8:

Love is patient, love is kind. It does not envy, it does not boast, it is not proud. It is not rude, it is not self-seeking, it is not easily angered, it keeps no record of wrongs. Love does not delight in evil but rejoices with the truth. It always protects, always trusts, always hopes, always perseveres. Love never fails.

Love in Action

Love is Patient

My family was on a trip to Disney World in Orlando, Florida. Our flight was on time as we took off from Baltimore. We hopped off the plane in Orlando as happy as could be. We were almost there! The kids were in a good mood, getting along, and excited for the upcoming trip. Everything was on time, and we got to Florida quicker than expected. Then something happened during one of our last steps of the process. We got to the baggage claim, and an announcement came over the speaker: "Due to storms in the area, the workers cannot retrieve luggage off the arriving planes at this time. We will provide updates as we learn more." We were so close to getting our luggage and moving on to our destination, Disney World! But there we sat for an hour and a half, waiting for storms to pass so we could retrieve our luggage. Remember the good moods and getting along I described earlier? They were no longer.

Paul Tripp (2017) describes love as, "Willing to have your life complicated by the needs and struggles of others without impatience or anger." Our days in leadership are filled with opportunities to practice patience as unexpected needs, struggles, and challenges appear all day, in our homes, at work, and wherever we may be. How are we responding in those moments? Like my kids (and I should certainly add myself), when things were going well on our trip to Orlando, it was easy to love and care for one another. It was easy to be patient when we didn't have to be patient. But when challenges arose, patience was one of the first things that left each of us, impacting the way we spoke and treated one another.

> It was easy to be patient when we didn't have to be patient. But when challenges arose, patience was one of the first things that left each of us, impacting the way we spoke and treated one another.

Are we showing love to others with patience, or do we lead impatiently, solely focused on ourselves and getting things done? Paul tells us in Ephesians, "Be completely humble and gentle; be *patient*, bearing with one another in love" (Ephesians 4:2). When I focus on my to-do list over people, the things I "need" to do and the places I "need" to be, the schedule I "need" to be on, I find myself responding (internally and externally) more impatiently to others when the needs of others arise, as I focus on my own needs and wants. That's not leadership. Leadership is patient.

Take Action

Patience is often in short supply in our world. Proverbs 14:29 says, "A patient man has great understanding, but a quick-tempered man displays folly." Be intentional about showing God's love to others by patiently responding to *every* situation. Pray that God would provide you with His never-ending supply of patience when it's needed most. We must be patient, bearing with one another in love (Ephesians 4:2).

Love is Kind

Thankfully, we did not lose our luggage during that flight to Orlando, but we began to lose a few other things. After we lost our patience, we started to lose something else: kindness towards one another. Growing up (and still to this day), my mom always says, "Attitude is everything." We want to focus on controlling the controllables and choosing an attitude of kindness to show love to those in our lives. Of course, our attitudes are certainly something within our control. In Galatians 5, Paul shares kindness as a fruit of the Spirit: "But the fruit of the Spirit is love, joy, peace, forbearance, *kindness*, goodness, faithfulness, gentleness and self-control" (Galatians 5:22-23). Notice the first fruit of the Spirit listed? *Love.* You are not just called to love others by being kind to the people who are kind to you, but you are called to be kind to everyone, and yes, that means even to those who are unkind to you.

Leading with kindness is easy when people are kind to us, but we must lead with a higher standard because leadership isn't about what is easy. The true reflection of our hearts is revealed as we lead and respond to those who are unkind to us and when the going gets difficult. We must clothe ourselves with kindness (Colossians 3:12). As the famous saying goes, "Be kind, for everyone you meet is fighting a hard battle." Leadership is kind. Be kind to one another.

> Leading with kindness is easy when people are kind to us, but we must lead with a higher standard because leadership isn't about what is easy.

Take Action

Ephesians 4:32 says, "Be kind and compassionate to one another, forgiving each other, just as in Christ God forgave you." Pray that God would continue to work on your heart to love others by treating them kindly. Focus on two things:

1. Surprise someone with an unexpected random act of kindness.
2. Choose to respond with kindness to those who are unkind to you.

Love Does Not Envy

I struggle with this one. I spend too much time looking around at what other people are doing instead of focusing my time and attention on who and what God has placed before me. This concept of envy is getting harder and more challenging with the increase in social media and the ability to be connected and see what others are doing at all times. Being envious of others accomplishes nothing and is a waste of time.

Leadership is about celebrating the successes of others. As leaders, we want to put others in positions to be successful and celebrate those successes. Leadership isn't about us being great. Leadership is bringing greatness out in others. Leadership is the pure, willful, sacrificial love concerned with the greatest good of others.

> Leadership isn't about us being great. Leadership is bringing greatness out in others.

And be careful; we can't get distracted by comparing ourselves to other leaders. An early leadership mistake I made and still struggle with today is comparing myself to other leaders, limiting my authentic self. A wise friend once told me, "Find your leadership voice, not somebody else's." When we compare ourselves to the successes of others, we miss out on our mission and the people we are called to lead, the ones standing right in front of us. Solomon says in Proverbs 14:30, "A heart at peace gives life to the body, but envy rots the bones." Leadership does not envy; leadership celebrates. Root for each other.

Love Does Not Boast, it is Not Proud

Leadership is humility, and Jesus is the great teacher of humility. Charles Spurgeon says the following about Jesus: "Is not this sentence the summary of His biography: '*He humbled himself*.'" Spurgeon continues, "A sense of Christ's amazing love for us has a greater tendency to humble us than even a consciousness of our own guilt" (2018). In *Leading with a Humble Heart*, I discuss how we are to lead with a heart of humble confidence - humble enough to know apart from Jesus, we can do nothing, but confident enough to know in Him, we can do all things (Bauermaster, 2022).

Jesus says in John Chapter 15, "I am the vine, you are the branches. If a man remains in me and I in him, he will bear much fruit, apart from me you can do nothing." Before leading with a humble heart, we must first humble ourselves. Peter tells us in 1 Peter 5:7, "Humble yourselves, therefore, under God's mighty hand, that he may lift you up in due time." When we are humbled by Christ's love for us, we can spread the love we receive, yet don't deserve, horizontally to others.

Humility is recognizing we are a branch, not the vine, to fruitfully lead others. Humility closes our mouth and opens our ears to listen to those around us. Humility says I'm sorry when we make a mistake. Humility asks for forgiveness when we have wronged others. Humility never stops learning and growing. We are to lead humbly in our roles by thinking of others before ourselves and putting their needs first.

Leadership is not about being the "hero." Instead, humble leadership is being the "guide" to put others in a position to be the "hero." Harry Truman said, "It is amazing what you can accomplish if you do not care who gets the credit" (Truman, n.d.). Solomon warns us many times in the book of Proverbs that pride goes before destruction (Proverbs 16:18). If you catch yourself becoming boastful or prideful, thinking you did something on your own, go to the foot of the cross. Christ's unconditional love for us should drive us toward humility. Leadership does not boast; it is not proud. Leadership is humility.

Take Action

Commit to humbly serving others in God's love. When the hour drew near for Jesus to face death on the cross, he washed his disciple's feet. John 13 tells us that Jesus got up from the meal, wrapped a towel around his waist, poured water into a basin, and began washing his disciple's feet (v.4-5). No matter what you face, look for a way to "wash the feet" of those around you. Choose to deny yourself and show Christ's love by serving others.

Love is Not Rude

Leadership is challenging; there's no reason to sugarcoat that. We have difficult conversations and interactions where people can undoubtedly be rude. But where there is love, our leadership has no space for rudeness. We ought to respond with kindness, gentleness, and goodness to others no matter what comes our way. Paul provides the blueprint in Titus 2: 7-8:

In everything, set them an example by doing what is good. In your teaching show integrity, seriousness, and soundness of speech that cannot be condemned, so that those who oppose you may be ashamed because they have nothing bad to say about us.

Paul uses the term "in everything." In everything, Paul? Yes. *In every* phone call, email, meeting, *every* face-to-face interaction with kids and adults, and in *every* conversation, we are to set an example of doing what is good through our integrity and soundness of speech—even when others are rude to us. That includes the conversations that no one can see. C.S. Lewis describes integrity as follows: "Integrity is doing the right thing, even when no one is watching" (Lewis, n.d.). Leadership is not rude; leadership sets the example of doing what is good.

Love is Not Self-Seeking

Did you ever have a coach or teacher growing up whom you wanted to perform well for? You didn't want to disappoint them, so you worked extra hard in the classroom, on the field, or court. I'm hoping you still have leaders in your life having that type of impact on you. As I reflect on those teachers and coaches now that I'm older, it wasn't about them; they weren't in it for themselves. They were invested in me, cared about me as a person, and wanted me, the class, or the team to succeed, whether in the classroom or in sports, and it showed by the way they put the class or team before themselves.

Leadership is not about me; leadership is not about you; it's about showing Christ's love to the people we lead. Leadership is wanting others to succeed, helping them succeed, and celebrating the successes. **In our leadership roles, we have a tremendous opportunity to be like Jesus serving as others-centered leaders instead of self-centered ones.** Matthew 19:30 says, "But many who are first will be last, and many who are last will be first." There's no room for self-seeking in leadership; it's all about putting others before ourselves. Leadership is not self-seeking; leadership is about the people we lead.

Love is Not Easily Angered

Leadership is steadfast, dutifully firm, and unwavering. We are called to be quick to listen, slow to speak, and slow to become angry (James 1:19). Unfortunately, we often get the verse wrong, and we are slow to listen, quick to speak, and quick to become angry. It's challenging to remain calm when we get an angry email, or someone curses at us. It's not easy when someone yells over the phone or a community member falsely accuses us of something. It's difficult to remain calm at home when there's a disagreement with our spouse or the kids are fighting after a long day. However, it's easy to be provoked into anger, become irritated, and get upset, but we don't want to do what is easy as leaders; we want to do what is right.

My administrative assistant is on the front lines of family, student, and staff interactions throughout the day. Whether face-to-face, by phone, or by email, her day is filled with unexpected requests and demands—it's the most challenging position in the building. She keeps a small note by her desk that says, *"Practice the pause! Proverbs 15:1: A gentle answer turns away wrath, but a harsh word stirs up anger."* What a great reminder for us all! We are called to be peacemakers (Matthew 5:9) and respond to others with gentleness. Luke tells us in Luke 6 to "Love your enemies, do good to those who hate you. Bless those who curse you, pray for those who mistreat you. Do to others as you would have them do to you" (Luke 6:27-28, 31). That's a hard standard to live up to, but that's what we are called to do. Psalm 103:8 says, "The Lord is compassionate and gracious, *slow to anger,* abounding in love." Leadership is not easily angered. Leadership is gentle; it is steadfast.

Take Action

Philippians 4:5 says, "Let your gentleness be evident to all; the Lord is near. Commit to showing God's love by responding to *every* situation with gentleness. Be aware of tense moments when it could be easy to react harshly to others. Write the following verse on a notecard and keep it by your desk, computer, or mirror: *A gentle answer turns away wrath, but a harsh word stirs up anger* (Proverbs 15:1). Be a leader in your home and work who responds with gentleness to others in all situations by how you speak and act. *Practice the pause!*

Love Keeps No Record of Wrongs

Don't keep score in your leadership and relationships. If you're struggling, holding on to grudges, and "keeping score" with others, remember that God's mercies are new for you every morning, they never come to an end. His love for you never stops; no matter what, He is faithful. We are to forgive much because we have been forgiven. Let that truth help you love others. Lamentations 3:22-23 is an excellent reminder of God's love for us and His new morning mercies:

The steadfast love of the Lord never ceases; his mercies never come to an end; they are new every morning; great is your faithfulness.

There should be no grudges in leadership. Every day is a fresh chance to start anew. Not just every day but every moment of every day. We can't hold on to the past as leaders; it will significantly impact the potential of our future. Clinging to the past prevents us and others from growing and moving into the future. Keeping a record of wrongs also greatly hinders our relationships

> We can't hold on to the past as leaders; it will significantly impact the potential of our future.

with one another and limits growth. Paul tells the Church in Ephesus, "Be kind and compassionate to one another, *forgiving each other*, just as Christ God forgave you (Ephesians 4:32). Leadership holds no record of wrongs; leadership forgives.

Love Always

A few sections earlier, we saw Paul use the term *"in everything."* Here we see him use the word always. The word always in this verse may be challenging for us to digest. We can protect, trust, hope, and persevere, but always? Spurgeon described it best, "Love does not ask to have an easy life of it: self-love makes that her aim. Love denies herself, sacrifices herself, that she may win victories for God" (Spurgeon, 1881). Simply put, far too often, our selfishness gets in the way of loving and leading those within our care as we should. Leaders must *always* protect, *always* trust, *always* hope, and *always* persevere. Always.

Summary

We love because God first loved us, and we are called to do everything in love (1 Corinthians 16:14). No matter what, we must trust God's unfailing love. As the principal told me, "The moment I could stop trying to be the 'perfect principal' and just focus on showing Christ's love…it all came together." Leadership is love.

> Be patient with people.
> Be kind to people.
> Seek the best interest of people.
> Be humble, and serve others.
> Keep no record of wrongs, and hold no grudges.
> Protect people, provide hope, and never give up on people.

That's leadership. That's love. As my wife says about parenting challenges: "We just need to keep showing up, keep loving them." No matter how challenging the work of leadership may seem, *keep showing up, and keep loving people.* Leadership is loving people.

CHAPTER 7

Encourage

Pillar #6 - Leadership is *encouraging* people.
"Therefore encourage one another and build
each other up, just as in fact you are doing."

1 Thessalonians 5:11

We all have those people in our lives who encourage us. They provide us with confidence, hope, and support. They are people we love to talk to or be around because they lift us up, fill us with confidence, cause us to think and reflect, and encourage us in our daily walk. We love to be in their presence. Not only do they encourage us in the moment, but they provide us with hope for the future. As you've read throughout this book, my life has been filled with encouragers, and my hope and prayer is that this book has encouraged you in your leadership roles.

It was a beautiful July Saturday morning as I sat with a leadership mentor on his front porch overlooking beautiful Pennsylvania farmland, enjoying an excellent breakfast of eggs and fruit. This mentor was not a school leader but a business owner, non-profit founder, and, most notably, a leader to his wife, grown children, and grandchildren.

As we met, we discussed life and leadership. I shared about upcoming job opportunities, potential interviews, and the impact the decisions could have on my family. I had been an assistant principal for the past four years, but I was now looking for a principal role and knew how important the decision would be for my family and me. I shared how uncertain I felt about everything, the various job opportunities, what was to come next, the impact on my family, whether I was at home enough, whether I was too invested in my work, would I make the wrong decisions, what would be the right decision, and so on and so forth. As you've found throughout this book, I still struggle. But guess what? I have *people* right beside me every step of the way.

During breakfast, I paused and thought about how God is always good. Only a few years prior, I was struggling with anxiety and depression, lost, and trying to figure out everything on my own. But there I sat, having breakfast on my mentor's porch, sharing praises and struggles, simply going through life *together*. I wasn't in it alone.

My mentor listened quietly, nodding his head slightly as I spoke. I could feel his wisdom and encouragement through his ability to listen. Next, he responded with a homework assignment and challenged me with the following (paraphrased):

> I'd like you to write two letters to yourself as if it's twenty years from now. Go ahead and write one letter as if you look back with regret. This letter will focus on poor decisions and the people impacted by those decisions. Next, write the other letter as if you made the right decisions. You look back over those twenty years on the solid decisions you made, and the people impacted the most. Maybe even try this: write the letters from your kids' perspective twenty years from now, as if they were sharing their experiences and memories of their childhood. Hold on to those letters and refer back to them when necessary.

I had my notebook, as I typically do when meeting with others, and quickly jotted down the wisdom. I didn't think much of it, but I wrote those two letters the next evening while my wife and kids were away. I decided to write the letters from the perspective of my oldest daughter, Olivia, who was nine at the time. The letters were written by her twenty-nine-year-old future self. As I sat there writing the letters, I was unexpectedly overcome by emotions. My two letters:

Letter of Regret

Dear Dad,

It's hard to believe I'm twenty-nine years old…wow, time moves quickly. I wanted to take some time to share some thoughts I've held onto over the years. You have been a good dad to us kids and husband to mom, but honestly, I wish you were around more as we grew up, both physically and mentally. Early on, you were always around, and we felt like the most special kids in the world: prayers, books, songs at night, lots of fun dad jokes, family TV shows, and family dinners. Then, there was a change. You pursued various jobs, thought about those jobs, and always seemed tired and distant at home. I could see Mom missing you as well. Too many nights, we went to bed without you home, and you were gone in the morning before we got up. There were too many times I heard Mom remind you that there were some changes you needed to make, and you would promise things would change, "It is just a busy season," you would say.

I didn't get to be around you nearly as much as I would have liked. You gave the best of you to everyone outside of our home. Eliot, Isaac, and I faced some challenging years; you seemed to be "half-present" when we needed you the most. I remember days that I just needed you to sit with me on the couch or stop by my room to check in, but you didn't; you were preoccupied with other things. I appreciate the times you were there, but it seemed like you were busy and had plenty of other things to do. We have a great family, and I've always been blessed with an incredible support system; whether it be grandparents, aunts, uncles, or family friends, they were always a tremendous support. However, it does not replace having our dad fully present in the home.

Please know that I love you; you have been successful in your career, provided for our family, and have impacted many, but I wanted to share where my heart is today. Now that I am grown, married to a wonderful husband, and have two kids, I want to be sure he pursues Jesus first and foremost, and secondly, he pursues our family. I've shared this with him many times about the challenges of growing up with a dad pursuing his career and the family taking a backseat. That is not what I want for my family.

Dad, thank you for sharing Jesus with us, especially early in our lives; without him, these earthly challenges would be even more challenging. We still need you, Dad, and so does Mom.

I love you.

Love,

Oliva

The Right Decisions Made

Dear Dad,

I can't believe I am twenty-nine years old. How quickly time flies! But Dad, I wanted to take time and write a letter to thank you. This is a letter thanking you for loving me, Eliot, Isaac, and, most of all, loving Mom. You truly showed Eliot and me how a wife should be loved by her husband. You made our family feel as if there was nothing more important than us, you never seemed too busy, and you were always fully present—even though I know God gave you many leadership responsibilities outside of the home. I'm thankful for your decisions with your various jobs, for always talking with Mom, and for putting our family's needs first. I know there were some decisions you could have made that may have helped you in your work career, but you humbly chose to put those decisions on hold for a more suitable time.

Thank you for the joy you and Mom brought to our home. I know there were many crazy years, messy rooms, toys everywhere, art supplies, snacks left out, fights in the car, dance, sports, and school events, but you focused on our hearts and pointed us to Jesus. We could clearly see that you and Mom were in it together. Please know we loved our childhood very much, lots of singing, dancing, bad dad jokes, funny sayings, coaching our teams, dance recitals, helping with homework, and "Daddy donut drives" in the car listening to praise and worship music. You were always there.

Now that I am grown and married with two kids, I thought this would be the time to share some of my thoughts with you. Dad, thank you for pursuing Jesus above anything else. It was evident in how you lived when we were kids and even more apparent today. I know I wouldn't admit it, but I always wanted to find a husband who loved me like you love mom and a husband who loved our kids like you have always loved the three of us. Thank you for prioritizing me; thank you for prioritizing our family. I pray my marriage can be like yours and Mom's. Thank you for the example you have set. God is good all the time!

I love you!

Love,

Olivia

In full transparency, I cry every time I read those two letters. Yes, I'm the one that wrote them, but I can feel and see how easily those words could come from my daughter. When I met with my mentor and wrote those letters, I had no idea the significant impact they would have on me, my life, and my family. He was *salt* and *light* in my life. That one-hour breakfast on my mentor's front porch encouraged me, not only in the moment, but daily, as I often refer to the conversation and the two letters. He encouraged me and encouraged my entire family and all the people I lead at work with one simple activity. We are called to encourage others in our leadership roles.

Encouragement Provides Hope

A fourth basic need emerging from Gallup's *why people follow* study was *hope* (Rath & Conchie, 2008). Those surveyed included words such as direction, faith, and guidance to best describe a leader who has had the most positive influence in their daily life. Rath and Conchie noted, "Hope gives followers something to look forward to, and it helps them see a way through complexity and chaos. When hope is absent, people lose confidence, disengage, and often feel helpless" (Rath & Conchie, 2008). That's what people along my path have done and are doing for me—they help me see my way through complexity and chaos while looking forward to the future.

Encourage People

A former school superintendent I served with would often say two words to me: "salt" and "light." Whether a text message, the end of a phone call, or leaving a face-to-face conversation, he would say, "Zac, salt and light." Similarly, when I left the house growing up, my dad always told my sisters and me, "Remember who you are and who you represent." He encouraged us to be salt and light in the world by pointing others to our Father in Heaven through how we lived our lives. Pointing others to Jesus by how we live is the greatest encouragement we can ever give someone.

When Jesus spoke to the disciples on the Sermon on the Mount, he told them: "You are the salt of the earth (Matthew 5:13)," followed shortly after by, "You are the light of the world (Matthew 5:14)." Not only that, Jesus tells them to let their light shine so others may see their good deeds and praise the Father in Heaven. Jesus tells us through His

Sermon on the Mount that we are to have an active, positive influence on the world around us.

We are called to be salt and light in the way we live our lives. As leaders, we have the tremendous opportunity to be salt and light in our homes, work, and beyond. We are surrounded by people daily in our roles, and we must serve and encourage others as salt and light. When we take the vertical relationship with our Heavenly Father and spread it horizontally to the people we lead, we lead with a heart that *encourages* people.

Pause and Take a Deep Breath

Read and reflect on these words from Jesus found in Matthew 5:13-16:

"You are the salt of the earth. But if the salt loses its saltiness, how can it be made salty again? It is no longer good for anything, except to be thrown out and trampled underfoot. You are the light of the world. A town built on a hill cannot be hidden. Neither do people light a lamp and put it under a bowl. Instead, they put it on its stand, and it gives light to everyone in the house. In the same way, let your light shine before others, that they may see your good deeds and glorify your Father in heaven."

How can these words from Jesus encourage you to be an encourager?

Encourage Like Barnabus

A friend reached out to me one afternoon with the following text message:

Joseph, a Levite from Cyprus, whom the apostles called Barna-bas (which means son of encouragement), sold a field he owned and bought the money and put it at the apostles' feet. Love this passage. He was such an encourager—and so selfless that disciples renamed him Barnabas.

Joseph was such an encouragement to those around him that the apostles began calling him Barnabas, meaning son of encouragement. Barnabas was the definition of encouragement and built a reputation for coming alongside people to support and provide hope in their life's journey.

Christians had been scattered by persecution, and Barnabas was sent to Antioch. When he arrived, he saw "the evidence of the grace of God, he was glad and encouraged them to all remain true to the Lord with all their hearts" (Acts 11:23). Barnabus was a *committed encourager*.

He lived out Jesus' calling to be *salt* and *light* as he was precious to those around him, preserved and protected, and enhanced their lives. Barnabas used his God-given light to illuminate the goodness of God to others. We should endeavor to be like Barnabas in our various leadership roles. *What if we all took on the "committed encourager" role in our leadership?* What a place our homes, schools, businesses, and organizations would be!

Encouragement in Action

Encourage as Salt

Let's begin by looking at the analogy of being salt in our leadership and the way we live our lives. We will look at salt's impact in three ways: 1) precious, 2) a preservative, and 3) adding flavor. We want to lead others in a precious, preserving, and flavorful way—in our homes and beyond.

Salt is Precious

Salt was a precious commodity in Jesus' day. It was such a valuable commodity that Roman soldiers were sometimes even paid with salt giving rise to the phrase "worth his salt." The definition of precious is "of great value, not to be wasted or treated carelessly" (Oxford Learner's Dictionaries, n.d.). Like salt, David reminds us in Psalm 139 what a precious commodity we are and why we are a precious commodity: "For you created my inmost being; you knit me together in my mother's womb. I praise you because I am fearfully and wonderfully made; your works are wonderful, I know that full well (v. 13 & 14). We are fearfully and wonderfully made by God, and we don't want to waste or treat our "saltiness" carelessly as we lead those within our care. *You are precious, and the people you lead are precious*–lead that way.

Take Action

You are "fearfully and wonderfully made." Be intentional about writing two letters to yourself as if it's ten or twenty years from now. Write one letter as if you look back with regret. This letter will focus on poor decisions and the people impacted by those decisions. Next, write the second letter as if the right choices were made. You will reflect on your wise decisions over those ten or twenty years and the people impacted the most. You can also write letters from your kids' or spouse's perspective as if they were sharing their experiences and memories of their childhood or relationship with you. Lastly, hold on to those letters and refer back to them when necessary.

Salt Preserves and Protects

Salt was used in ancient times to preserve meat and slow decay. We want to be the salt in our leadership that has a preserving influence on those around us, encouraging each other to keep going. Another way to say that salt preserves is that salt protects. In the last chapter, we focused on love and saw in 1 Corinthians 13 that love *always* protects. Salt is also used as a disinfectant that promotes healing. What a significant challenge, but more importantly, a significant opportunity for us as leaders to preserve and protect those we lead. We are to function like salt and be a preservative for others in our leadership roles and our world.

Take Action

Commit to only speaking words that build up and encourage others. Refrain from any gossip or negative talk. Paul tells us in Ephesians 4:29, "Do not let any unwholesome talk come out of your mouths, but only what is helpful for building others up according to their needs, that it may benefit those who listen."

Before you speak, whether to someone or about someone, are the words about to come out of your mouth helpful in building others up, or do they tear others down?

An entire forest can be set on fire by a spark and a large ship can be steered by a small rudder (James 3:4-5). The tongue is small but powerful. Preserve and protect others through your words. Use your tongue to encourage and build others up.

Salt Adds Flavor

A more modern-day use of salt is for adding flavor. One of my favorite meals is a cheeseburger and french fries. I don't know about you, but I usually begin by adding more salt to the fries and burger, even though the meal is already salty. I do the same thing with another one of my favorite meals, a steak and baked potato. Why? Because the salt adds flavor–it makes it better (at least for me, anyway). We should seek to be salt and add flavor to the lives around us through our encouragement. We should enhance the lives of others by being a blessing to the people around us.

Lastly, I'm typically extremely thirsty after that cheeseburger and french fry meal. Sometimes no matter how much water I drink, it feels like it's never enough. Do people thirst for Jesus and the love of Christ because of your leadership influence?

Take Action

Pray and ask God to lay someone on your heart who could use a word of encouragement. As a name comes to you, simply take thirty seconds to send them a text message of encouragement, letting them know that you are thinking and praying for them. Add flavor to their life through your encouragement and let God take it from there.

Encourage as Light

You may have heard the song "Fancy Like" by Walker Hayes (2021) and maybe even seen the TikTok dance with Walker and his daughter on their front porch. "Yeah, we fancy like Applebees on a date night..." The song reached #3 on the Billboard Hot 100 and #1 on the Hot Country Songs chart, becoming one of the fastest platinum-certified singles of 2021. But this isn't about all that; this is about Craig. Craig? Unlike "Fancy Like," many people don't know about a song that Walker released in 2018 called "Craig." If you YouTube the song "Fancy Like," you will find 128 million views (as of July 2023). Craig, on the other hand, has just over 842,000 views. Still impressive, but nothing compared to the 127 million views of "Fancy Like."

When you dive into Walker's career and hear him share his story you learn that he was struggling when he met Craig. Walker had been dropped by two record labels; his musical career was fading, he was struggling with alcohol addiction, and he lost a child at birth. The husband and father of six was broke and needed help. It was the lowest point in Walker's life.

That's when Walker met a man named Craig. You can listen to the whole song and how Craig and his wife helped Walker and his family, but I want to point out a few lines of the song that Walker wrote about Craig.

> Now he's not the light of the world,
> but I wish my light was as bright as his.
> Yeah he just might be tight with a man that is

That's encouragement. Craig never left Walker and his family during this time of need and, as the song shares, even gave the family a car. He walked alongside Walker and his family step by step during their darkest hour. When writing the song, Walker was an atheist; he didn't believe in God and had no hope for the future. But as the lyrics explain, Walker noticed something about Craig—he wasn't the light of the world, but he saw a "light" in Craig and wished his light could shine as bright as his. Craig's vertical relationship with his Heavenly Father illuminated the goodness of God horizontally to Walker.

We all need "Craigs" in our lives, and we all need to be "Craigs" in the lives of others. Maybe you can think of a few "Craigs" in your life; I know I can. You've read about many of them throughout this book. Those are people who are there for you with encouragement no matter what you're going through or where you are in life. They keep you pushing forward one step at a time, walking alongside you, and they never leave your side.

As we continue to reflect on the Sermon on the Mount, Jesus also told the disciples, "You are the light of the world." Jesus said in John 8:12, "I am the light of the world. Whoever follows me will not walk in darkness, but will have the light of life." Not only does Jesus say He is the light of the world, but He also tells us that we are the light of the world. What a great compliment and responsibility to serve as God's ambassadors, living as light in a dark and hurting world. Psalm 119:105 says, "Your word is a lamp unto my feet and a light unto my path." We are both light-receivers, receiving light from our Heavenly Father guiding our path as we walk, and light givers, passing the vertical light from God horizontally to those we lead.

Light Provides Safety

When I think of the impact of light, I can't help but think of bedtime with my young kids. I've heard it many times across the hallway, "Daddy...Daddy..." Other times my kids will startle me by walking into my room, standing beside my bed, and staring at me. Just because they're scared doesn't mean they have to scare me! Ever been there before? All joking aside, I walk to my kids' room to check what may be wrong. "I'm scared and can't fall asleep. It's too dark in here." At that point, typically, two things are likely to occur. Sometimes I will try to locate a nightlight or leave the hallway light on outside their room to provide actual light. Many times the light is sufficient for them, and I tuck them into bed (for the fifth or sixth time), and they fall right asleep with the comfort of the additional light on. That light provides them with a sense of security and safety.

Other times, I quickly learn that it is not the actual light they want. I will go into my five-year-old son's room, and he will say, "It's too dark; I'm scared." Other times he won't even call out, and he will sneak into my room at night and sleep on the floor beside my bed. Even though there is already a nightlight on or light shining in from the hallway bathroom, I know my son wants the comfort of his parents lying beside him. It's not the physical light he wants; it's the light my wife and I provide as his parents that gives him peace, safety, and comfort to fall asleep. One morning I awoke to my son lying on the floor beside my bed, curled up in his blanket. I didn't notice him at first and stepped right on him! Later that morning, I asked him why he came to our room in the middle of the night. He said, "My room was too dark." My oldest daughter chimed in and said, "Isaac, that doesn't make sense; their room is darker than yours." He responded, "Well, their room has Mommy and Daddy." A little light in a dark room can make a big difference. We are called to be that light in leadership, providing peace, safety, and security to those we lead.

Take Action

Encouragement is letting others know you are in their corner with them. Be intentional about noticing and celebrating the work of others. It doesn't have to be anything elaborate. Let others know you see their hard work, they are important to you, and their efforts matter. Encourage others by showing them that they are valued and appreciated. A simple "Thank you" and "Well done" can go a long way in encouraging others. Someone in your life may need to hear four simple words: "I'm proud of you."

Light Illuminates the Goodness of our Heavenly Father

We should seek to let our lights shine in our leadership roles. Our lights don't do much good if we keep them hidden and don't allow them to shine. We are called to let our lights shine brightly at all times.

Unfortunately, doubt and uncertainty often try to creep in and fill our minds, preventing our God-given lights from shining brightly. It is selfish of us to keep our light hidden, and we must have a more significant concern for others and shine our light on them.

Letting our lights shine does not mean that people see the good in us, but that our light reflects the good of our Heavenly Father. Charles Spurgeon said, "To be the light of the world surrounds life with the most stupendous responsibilities...The object of our shining is not that men may see how good we are, nor even see us at all, but that they may see grace in us and God in us, and cry, 'What a Father these people must have"(Spurgeon, 1873). We have such a tremendous opportunity in leadership because we are surrounded by so many people facing darkness, difficulties, and hardships. Light is used to illuminate, and we can't let fear hold us back, hiding our lights and missing out on passing the vertical love of God horizontally to those we lead. Try this exercise. You may or may not have heard the children's song "This Little Light of Mine" (Odetta, 1962). When you get to the blank, I want you to fill in the people or places that you lead:

This little light of mine, I'm gonna let it shine. This little light of mine, I'm gonna let it shine. This little light of mine, I'm gonna let it shine. Let it shine, let it shine, let it shine.

Everywhere I go, I'm gonna let it shine. Everywhere I go, I'm gonna let it shine. Everywhere I go, I'm gonna let it shine. Let it shine, let it shine, let it shine.

Shine it all over _____, I'm gonna let it shine, Shine it all over

_____, I'm gonna let it shine, Shine it all over _____, I'm gonna let it shine, let it shine, let it shine.

Take Action

Rest in knowing you serve a God who is the light of the world—He is where your light comes from. Jesus said in John 8:12, "I am the light of the world. Whoever follows me will not walk in darkness, but will have the light of life." Not only does Jesus say *He* is the light of the world, he tells us that *we* are the light of the world. What a great compliment and responsibility to serve as God's ambassadors, living as light in a dark and hurting world. Rest in him.

Summary

We must live out the figures of salt and light in our leadership. Encourage people with your words and actions. Help others through complexity and chaos, providing them with a bright hope for the future. When you can encourage someone, do it—*never waste an unspoken blessing.* We are called to be aware of the needs of those around us and how we can *encourage* and build them up. As Paul says in Ephesians 4:29, "Do not let any unwholesome talk come out of your mouths, but *only what is helpful for building others up according to their needs, that it may benefit* those who listen." Ask yourself: "How can I add value to someone else's life?" as you start each day. There are already enough fault-finders in the world; encourage one another and build each other up (1 Thessalonians 5:11)! We must commit to encouraging and building each other up. Leadership is encouraging people.

CHAPTER 8

The *Leading with PEOPLE* 7 x 7 Action Plan

This 49-day *Leading with PEOPLE* Action Plan will help you implement the key pillars of the PEOPLE Framework in your daily life. Why 49 days? The PEOPLE Framework begins with building the foundation and is followed by the six letters in the word PEOPLE for seven weeks. The foundation and each pillar walk you through seven days for a total of 49. The purpose is to lead *with* people one day at a time focusing on the foundation and the key pillars of the framework. The action plan combines bringing people alongside you in your leadership and fruitfully leading others.

What you'll notice as you read and begin to implement the 7 x 7 *Leading with PEOPLE* Action Plan:

- You saw many of these action items throughout the "Take Action" sections of each chapter. They are now written for you to follow in a guided day-by-day format. For example, the first week is seven days focused on building and strengthening your foundation. Week two then begins with Prioritize, Week three Empathize, etc.

+ Please note: **never stop building and strengthening your foundation.** Look to pray and memorize scripture daily to align your heart with God's heart throughout the plan. Where your treasure is, there your heart will be also (Matthew 6:21). We want to treasure what God treasures.

+ You can implement this plan in different areas of your life at different times. You may need to work through the action plan focusing on your family. Others may navigate the action plan focusing on people at work. Some of you may implement pieces of the action plan simultaneously at work and at home. You may have a struggling relationship in your life or a relationship you are looking to strengthen. Focus the entire plan on that person. It could be your spouse, a child, or a close friend. The plan is all about being intentional in our relationships—*with* God and *with* people.

+ The first day of each week is typically focused on a scripture passage, and the last day is focused on rest. Take advantage of these days. They are essential in preparing your heart for each week and closing out each week.

+ You are fearfully and wonderfully made. God made you different from anyone else. Bring yourself and your personality into the action plan.

+ I recommend journaling and reflecting on your journey. How do you see God working in your life and the lives of the people around you?

+ The *Leading With People Action Plan* is building our foundation of aligning our hearts with God and walking day-by-day, side-by-side, with the people we lead. It's quiet, humble leadership in the lives of one another.

Now, go and humbly lead *with* people.

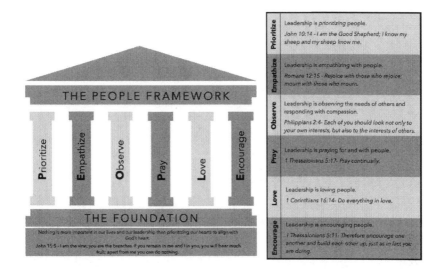

Week 1

The Foundation

Nothing is more important in our lives and our leadership
than prioritizing our hearts to align with God's heart.

Day 1 - Pray Continually

As we look to build and strengthen our foundation, today's challenge is
to simply pray. Focus on the two words found in 1 Thessalonians 5:17,
"pray continually." Not only by praying in the morning but, as the verse
says, "continually." Pray throughout the day. Feel free to set multiple
alarms on your phone as a reminder to pray. And don't worry about
praying the perfect prayer; there's no such thing. Open your heart to
God, praying for strength, wisdom, guidance, and discernment in your
leadership journey. Ask Him what you should pray for as you humbly

pray (John 15:5), *"You are the vine, I am the branch, apart from you I can do nothing, but in you I can bear much fruit. Help me bear fruit, I need you, I can't do it on my own."*

As Jesus tells us in Matthew, "Ask and it will be given to you: seek and you will find; knock and the door will be opened to you. For everyone who asks receives; he who seeks finds; and to him who knocks, the door will be opened (v. 7-8). God doesn't promise this life will be easy, but He promises that He is right there with us every step of the way.

Day 2 - Memorize God's Word

In addition to praying, commit to memorizing scripture; make studying God's word part of your daily routine. Begin with Bible verses or passages that are meaningful to you, the season of life you're in, the situation you're facing, or an area with which you're struggling. I don't know what you're going through or what God is preparing you for in your leadership, but find a verse that hits close to home in the season of life you are in. As you begin to memorize verses, it's not about quantity; it's about quality. Take your time as you fill your heart with God's wisdom. As you memorize a verse, study the context of the passage as well. What is the meaning behind the verse?

Write the Bible verse on a slip of paper and keep it in your pocket as a reminder throughout the day. As Paul says in Philippians, "Finally, brothers, whatever is *true*, whatever is *right*, whatever is *pure*, whatever is *noble*, whatever is *lovely*, whatever is *admirable* - if anything is *excellent* or *praiseworthy* - think about such things" (Philippians 4:8). Filling your heart and mind with those words described by Paul comes from reading the Bare Word of God. God's word is a lamp to your feet and light for your path (Psalm 119:105).

Day 3 - Treasure

In addition to praying and memorizing scripture, spend quiet time journaling a list of the current treasures in your life. Who or what treasure are you seeking? Examine your heart and note how the treasures you list impact your daily life and leadership. Be honest in your reflections. Do the treasures help you run the race God has marked out for you? Or do they get in the way of being more like Jesus? Remember, your heart will follow what you treasure and overflow in how you treat others. For where your treasure is, there your heart will be also (Matthew 6:21). In Jesus is where you find your worth, your identity.

Day 4- Lead from Overflow

In addition to praying and memorizing scripture, quietly reflect on when you are living and leading at your best. Create a T-chart, and at the top of one column, write "Overcommitted." On the top of the other column, write "Overflow." Next, create a list under each column of when you are leading from a place of overcommitment and when you're leading from a place of overflow. Commit to building your foundation under the items listed under "Overflow." Use the following bullet points as a guide:

+ When do you feel and operate at your best?
+ What rejuvenates you, and what drains you?
+ Who are the people who rejuvenate you, and who are the people who drain you?
+ What do you need to say no to?
+ What must you say yes to?

Day 5 - Who's Coming with You?

In addition to prayer and memorizing scripture, spend time reflecting on who you can surround yourself with as part of your foundation. Focus your prayer on whom you can reach out to as a mentor in your life. Ask God to bring someone into your life who would be willing to invest in you. Is there someone you can mentor? They may already be right in front of you. Not only seek to bring a mentor into your life but commit to mentoring someone else. The timing may not be right now, but keep your eyes open. Reach out to those people and open up. Joshua had Moses; Elisha had Elijah, Timothy had Paul; who's coming with you?

Day 6 - Prepare to Step Outside Your Comfort Zone

In addition to praying and memorizing scripture, identify a comfort zone that is holding you back from maximizing your God-given gifts and abilities. Create a list of doubts and fears currently consuming brain space. Is it something as "simple" as opening up to a trusted friend about something in your life? Find a quiet space to listen to the song "No Longer Slaves" by Bethel Music (Case, J., Helser, J., Johnson, B., 2015). Turn each of those doubts and fears into prayer and ask God to fill you with His confidence, not your own. Rip the list up and throw it out. Step out of your doubts and fears and step into your calling. Where is God calling you to step outside your comfort zone? Turn it over to Him.

Day 7 - Rest

Rest, quietness, stillness, and trust are beautiful words. This one may be the hardest of all for you: simply being still, resting in God's provisions. David said in Psalm 23, "The Lord is my shepherd, I shall not be in want. He makes me lie down in green pastures, he leads me beside quiet waters" (v. 1-2). Lie down in those green pastures, and walk beside those quiet waters; God is your shepherd, and you have all that you need. Rest in what God has done for you, is doing for you, and will do for you; He is in control. Take a deep breath and picture Jesus saying to you, "Come to me _____, you are weary and burdened, I will give you rest."

Week 1 Reflections

_____

_____

_____

_____

_____

_____

_____

_____

_____

_____

_____

_____

_____

_____

_____

_____

_____

_____

_____

_____

Week 2

Prioritize

Pillar #1 - Leadership is Prioritizing People

Day 1 - The Good Shepherd

Today, spend time reading the passage below found in John 10. As you read, reflect on Jesus as your Good Shepherd:

I am the good shepherd. The good shepherd lays down his life for the sheep. The hired hand is not the shepherd who owns the sheep. So when he sees the wolf coming, he abandons the sheep and runs away. Then the wolf attacks the flock and scatters it. The man runs away because he is a hired hand and cares nothing for the sheep. I am the good shepherd; I know my sheep, and my sheep know me - just as the Father knows me, and I know the Father - and I lay down my life for the sheep (v. 11-15).

How can Jesus as your Good Shepherd impact your daily walk and leadership to those in your care?

Day 2 - Be Where Your Feet Are

Today, commit to being where your feet are—put your phone down and look up for the "little" moments. Be intentional about being present with the people right in front of you. Don't allow your phone to pull you from the people directly in your presence. Commit to not only putting your phone down but putting it away. *Be where your feet are,* present and fully engaged with the people you lead. You don't want to miss the precious people and moments all around you. Be purposeful in noticing the "little" moments you wouldn't have typically noticed with your eyes glued to your phone.

149

Day 3 - Greet People Like They are Special to You–Because They Are

Be purposeful in how you greet others today. Make others feel like they are special by the way you greet them. It could be something as simple as a handshake, fist bump, or a smile at work. Maybe it's a kiss or hug to your family members as they wake up or you arrive home from work. It doesn't have to be a grand gesture; show people you are grateful they are in your life by putting a little extra effort into how you greet them. Remember, people won't always remember what you said or did, but they will remember how you made them feel (Angelou, n.d).

Day 4 - Call People by Name

Today, strive to show people you genuinely care for them by calling them by name. Do this, remembering that God has called *you* by name; you are His (Isaiah 43:1). Whether face-to-face, on the phone, by email, or by text message, put in a little extra effort by prioritizing using the person's name. It's just a little thing that can go a big way.

Do you struggle with names? Spend today focused on being intentional with learning names. Try a few of these suggestions:

1. Be confident. Change the mindset of "I'm bad with names."
2. When you meet someone, actually pause and listen to their name. Too often, we forget a person's name one second after hearing them say it because we weren't actually listening.
3. Repeat someone's name back to them sparingly throughout a conversation after meeting them.
4. Make name associations in your head to draw on connections as you meet someone.

5. If you forget a name, don't allow the awkwardness to continue. Say something like, "Can you tell me your name one more time?"

Day 5 - Healthy People

Brainstorm and implement one way you can create a culture of healthy people in your home or organization. You can't live out the mission and vision of your home or organization if your people aren't healthy or burnt out, and operating less than their best. We want our families and all the people we lead to be healthy. Take a step back and reflect: What's a barrier that you could remove to help others work towards the mission in a healthy way? What can you remove from someone's plate today? What can you say no to for yourself and for the good of others?

Day 6 - Prioritize Your Most Precious Crop

Choose to prioritize your family today. This could be your spouse, kids, and anyone else you consider family. In a society where things at work come home, and things at home go to work, commit to devoting all your time and attention to your family. Plan a family date or maybe even a family getaway. Maybe your family has been so busy you must prioritize slowing down and enjoying quality time together at home. Sit down at the table and enjoy a home-cooked meal, gather around the table for a game, share some laughs, enjoy a good dessert, and get outside to do something active together. Make memories together with your most precious crop–your family.

Day 7 - Rest

Sorry to say this, but you *can't do it all*. Choose to rest today. God tells Moses in Exodus 34:21, "Six days you shall labor, but on the seventh day you shall rest; even during the plowing season and harvest you must rest." You may be thinking there is far too much to do to stop and rest. Trust that God knows best and that he will intercede for you, even during your "busy" seasons. Take a step back and reflect on how you saw God work this week in your life and the lives of those around you. You will be better for it.

Week 2 Reflections

_____

_____

_____

_____

_____

_____

_____

_____

_____

_____

_____

_____

_____

_____

_____

_____

_____

_____

_____

_____

_____

_____

_____

Week 3

Empathy

Pillar #2 - Leadership is Empathizing with People

Day 1 - Jesus Wept

Today, commit to reading about the death of Lazarus in John 11. The shortest verse of the Bible can be found in verse 35: "Jesus wept." These two simple words carry great significance. They are powerful and insightful, filled with great hope. Jesus spent thirty-three years on this earth; He knows and understands your grief. We serve a God who cares about your sorrows and empathizes with you. He cares about our tears and we are called to care about the tears of one another. Lead with empathy, trusting that we serve a compassionate God who will one day wipe away every tear.

Day 2 - God, Give Me Your Eyes

Ask God to open your eyes to the needs and celebrations around you today. Romans 12:15 says, "Rejoice with those who rejoice and mourn with those who mourn." Too often, we are unaware of who is rejoicing and who is mourning as we navigate each day. We see through our lens, from our past, from our experiences–blinding us to the needs of the people we lead. Take four minutes and listen to Brandon Heath's song, "Give Me Your Eyes." As you listen to the song think about your family, those at work, and strangers passing that you haven't even met. Celebrate and grieve with one another. Turn the chorus of the song into your prayer for today and every day:

Give me Your eyes for just one second
Give me Your eyes so I can see
Everything that I keep missin'
Give me Your love for humanity
Give me Your arms for the broken-hearted
The ones that are far beyond my reach
Give me Your heart for the ones forgotten
Give me Your eyes so I can see

Day 3 - Tell Your Story

Pause and take a deep breath; you have a story. You have a story that you need to share with someone. A story that will strengthen you and the person or people you share it with. Begin today by praying God would point you to where you can share it. Today may be the day you share your story; today may be the first step in preparing to share your story. When we share our stories, our eyes and hearts are opened to the stories around us. You'll be amazed. Don't keep your story hidden. To tell others your story is to tell of God and what He has done and is doing in your life. As you prepare to tell your story, pray and listen to Big Daddy Weave's (Beihl, B., Redmon, J., Shirk, J., Weaver, M., 2015) song, "My Story." There are too many hidden stories; share yours. Someone needs it.

Day 4 - Ask for Help

Not only do we need to ask God to open our eyes to the needs around us, we need to be intentionally intrusive in each other's lives to help us see clearly. Today, pray that God would guide you in reaching out to a close friend for help. Reaching out to others for help is never easy, but it's necessary. Is there a situation you're struggling to see clearly and need someone to hand you a pair of "glasses" by offering their perspective? It's OK admitting you can't do it alone; ask for help. You'll see better.

Day 5 - Purposefully Slow Down

Empathy is enhanced when we slow down and use our time to show people we are happy to give them the time they need and deserve. Today, commit to slowing down. Leaders can be so "busy" that we often forget to slow down, pause, and look up. Literally, be cognizant of slowing down as you drive. If you usually drive in the left lane on the highway, drive in the right lane. Allow cars to whiz right by. As you drive slower, notice things around you becoming more clear. Praise God in traffic or when you get stopped at a red light. What a great reminder for us that we are not in control—to slow down and come to a complete stop.

Purposefully walk slower in your homes and at work. Is there a family member, a spouse, or a child who needs you to stop into their room to ask how their day was or if everything is OK? Do you need to sit on the couch and talk with your spouse? Is there a co-worker or employee who needs you to stop by their office or classroom to check in and see how they're doing? Does someone in your life need your help? Quit being in such a hurry. Purposefully slow down; don't miss that moment by speeding right on by.

Day 6 - Ask Empathetic Questions and Listen

Today, seek to ask empathetic questions to others. Leaders often think we need to have the correct answers when we should focus instead on asking the right questions, listening, and learning to discern the needs of others. Skip over the basic questions like, "How are you" or "How is your day going?" The relationship you have with others will impact their responses to the questions. Try one or a few of the following questions:

- What is the biggest challenge you're facing today?
- What is the most challenging thing you have to do this week?
- What is something coming up that you are looking forward to?

It's easy to walk right on by with a "How are you?" It takes effort to ask insightful, empathetic questions and listen intently to the response. Listen for ways that you can help or provide support. These questions help set the stage for compassion—observing the needs of others and moving into action.

Day 7- Rest

It's OK to rest; really, it is. Today, commit to resting in God's provisions by taking a nap. Read Genesis 2:2-3: "By the seventh day God had finished the work he had been doing; so on the seventh day, he rested from all his work. Then God blessed the seventh day and made it holy, because on it he rested from all the work of creating he had done." Enjoy the sweet rest from your Heavenly Father today.

Week 3 Reflections

_____

_____

_____

_____

_____

_____

_____

_____

_____

_____

_____

_____

_____

_____

_____

_____

_____

_____

_____

_____

_____

_____

_____

Week 4

Observe

Pillar #3 - Leadership is Observing the Needs of Others and Responding with Compassion

Day 1 - The Good Samaritan

Today, commit to reading the Parable of the Good Samaritan found in Luke 10: 25-37:

On one occasion an expert in the law stood up to test Jesus. "Teacher," he asked, "what must I do to inherit eternal life?"

"What is written in the Law?" he replied. "How do you read it?"

He answered, "Love the Lord your God with all your heart and with all your soul and with all your strength and with all your mind; and, 'Love your neighbor as yourself.'"

"You have answered correctly," Jesus replied. "Do this and you will live."

But he wanted to justify himself, so he asked Jesus, "And who is my neighbor?"

In reply Jesus said: "A man was going down from Jerusalem to Jericho, when he was attacked by robbers. They stripped him of his clothes, beat him and went away, leaving him half dead. A priest happened to be going down the same road, and when he saw the man, he passed by on the other side. So too, a Levite, when he came to the place and saw him, passed by on the other side. But a Samaritan, as he traveled, came where the man was; and when he saw him, he took pity on him. He went to him and bandaged his wounds, pouring on oil and wine. Then he put the man on his own donkey, brought him to an inn and took care of him. The next day he took out two denarii and gave them to the innkeeper. 'Look after him,' he said, 'and when I return, I will reimburse you for any extra expense you may have.' Which of these three do you think was a neighbor to the man who fell into the hands of robbers?"

The expert in the law replied, "The one who had mercy on him."

Jesus told him, "Go and do likewise."

Don't be like the priest and Levite crossing to the other side of the road when you see someone in need. Be like the Good Samaritan who showed mercy and compassion. As Jesus said, "Go and do likewise."

Day 2 - Make a Phone Call

God's timing is perfect. Pray and ask God to open your eyes and heart to someone you can call today as a "small" act of compassion. Show God's compassionate grace through genuine words to others. As you're on the phone, focus on being a listening ear for that person. The phone call may be all they need, or through the conversation, you'll discern additional ways they need your help.

Day 3 - Let Someone Know You're Right There with Them

Today, ask God to make you more aware of situations where you could come alongside others with comfort and support. Choose to pause and reflect on who needs to know that "you are right there with them." Don't incorrectly assume that the people you lead are right there with you, and that you're right there with them. Are you trying to lead out in front, expecting others to follow when what they need is for you to slow down, observe their needs, and respond with compassion? Come alongside people and meet them "where they are." Remember, compassion doesn't have to be a grand gesture; it can be a literal or metaphorical hug. It only takes a minute to pause and let someone around us know we see them, we empathize with them, and we're there for them.

Day 4 - Drop What You're Doing

Today, ask God to prepare your heart and open your eyes to the immediate needs around you. Be intentional about dropping whatever you are doing to help someone in need. You can show God's compassion to others through unexpected gestures of kindness. It may be someone you don't even know. Keep your heart and eyes open today.

Day 5 - Stack Stones

Who do you know or who have you seen facing difficulties right now that you could help? We need to walk alongside each other, stacking stones, remembering the compassion God shows us and the great things He has done so we can show compassion to others. Choose to "stack stones" with someone today or schedule it for the near future. Arrange to spend time with them. It may be for coffee, breakfast, lunch, a workout, or something that works for the two of you. It's possible the person you need to stack stones with is right there in your house. Whichever route you choose, focus on these four questions:

1. Name the trial: literally name the difficult season in your life.
2. Create a list of Bible passages and verses that guided you through the trial.
3. Reflect on how God brought you through the trial, how God saw you through it.
4. What did you learn about God during the trial, and what did you learn about yourself?

Day 6 - Take a Step of Faith

Today, choose to take a step of faith. Begin in prayer, asking God to strengthen you with His wisdom, guidance, and discernment. Is there something that's been on your heart that you're ready to act upon? It could be an idea for starting a non-profit organization, going on a mission trip, organizing a fundraiser event, or traveling a long distance to see a friend or family member you haven't seen in a while. Is there a broken relationship in your life in which you need to choose to show God's grace and compassion? Be bold and courageous; take a step of faith.

Day 7 - Rest

Be intentional about resting in God's goodness today. Read, study, and memorize Isaiah 63:7: *"I will tell of the kindnesses of the Lord, the deeds for which he is to be praised, according to all the Lord has done for us—yes, the many good things he has done for the house of Israel, according to his compassion and many kindnesses."* Pause and reflect on the compassion, grace, and mercy God shows you. Let that drive the way you compassionately live and lead daily.

Week 4 Reflections

_____

_____

_____

_____

_____

_____

_____

_____

_____

_____

_____

_____

_____

_____

_____

_____

_____

_____

_____

_____

_____

_____

_____

Week 5

Pray

Pillar #4 - Leadership is Praying for and with People

Day 1 - Ask God to Be Your Helper

Pour out your heart to God in prayer; cry out to Him. Don't let your finite mind limit the Almighty God. Ask God to be your helper in each leadership role you serve. How many ways can you fill in the following blank?

God, help me as a _____.

What various roles do you serve that you need to hand over to God? Maybe you don't even know where to start. If so, try praying, *"God, I lift my eyes to you. I don't know what or who to pray for, but my help comes from you, the One who made the heavens and the earth. Show me the needs around me; open my eyes, Lord. Be my helper."*

Remember, God doesn't desire the perfect prayer; He desires your heart. Pour out your heart to God and watch Him work.

Day 2 - Keep a "Little Black Book"

Today, commit to keeping a prayer notebook. When we get to know the people we lead, we learn their stories, and we can respond with compassion. We can then lift those people up in prayer. It certainly doesn't have to be a little black book, but find a book or journal to keep a list of the needs, struggles, and celebrations of the people you lead. The book will be a valuable resource to guide your prayer life.

Secondly, use the book to follow up and check in on those people. It can also be beneficial to write specific dates within the book. Are there milestones, such as one month, six months, or a year after a difficulty for someone you know, where you can reach out, write a card, or just let them know you are praying for them? Was there an important doctor's appointment that you could follow up on? You can add those to your calendar as a friendly reminder. It doesn't have to only be hardships, either. Did a staff member get married? Have a child? Be sure to jot those items down in the notebook as well.

Day 3 - Pray for Others

Today, choose to pray for others throughout the day. Use your "little black book" as a guide. We are called to be devoted to prayer, watchful, and thankful (Colossians 4:2). We must be in constant and loyal prayer. Prayer is not meant to be an event only performed at certain times, but prayer is to be an ongoing dialogue with the Lord. As you walk through your day, praise God for the people in your life. Pray for the people inside your home, pray for friends and family, pray for others throughout your day. We are to pray continually (1 Thessalonians 5:17).

Day 4 - Pray with Someone

Today may stretch you outside of your comfort zone. Pray *with* someone today. Ask God to place someone on your heart who could use the encouragement of praying together. This could be your spouse, your children, another family member, or someone outside of your home. Encourage and build them up through prayer today.

Day 5 - Find a Prayer Partner

We can't do it alone; we are made to be in community. Pray that God would place a prayer partner on your heart, someone you can navigate life with through prayer on a consistent basis. Maybe you already have one. How could having a prayer partner enhance your prayer life and daily walk? We can encourage and support each other as we pray for each other's needs and turn every blessing back into praise. Jesus tells us in Matthew 18:20, "For where two or three come together in my name, there I am with them." Carry each other's burdens and stand in the gap for one another as you boldly go out in God's confidence. Remember, Jesus sent his disciples out 2 x 2.

Day 6 - Turn Your Worry List Into a Prayer List

Today, choose to turn all your worries into prayer. Be intentional about memorizing Philippians 4:6: *"Do not be anxious about anything, but in everything, by prayer and petition, with thanksgiving, present your requests to God."* As you feel your anxiousness or worry on the rise, do the following:

1. Pause and acknowledge your worries, fears, and uncertainties.
2. Write "Worry List" at the top of a paper or journal page.
3. List everything overwhelming you with worry.
4. Return to the top of the paper and cross out the word "Worry."
5. Recite Philippians 4:6 - *"Do not be anxious about anything, but in everything, by prayer and petition, with thanksgiving, present your requests to God."*
6. Replace the word "Worry" with "Prayer."
7. Turn the worry list over to God in prayer.
8. Over the next week, month, or beyond, look back over the prayer list—what do you notice?

Day 7 - Rest

Choose to be an unhurried leader today. Be intentional about slowing down and enjoying God and the relationships He has placed in your life. Reflect on all that Jesus has done for you. David says in Psalm 31:19, "How great is your goodness, which you have stored up for those who fear you, which you bestow in the sight of men on those who take refuge in you." Find rest and refuge in God's goodness today, considering the great things He has done for you (1 Samuel 12:23).

_____

_____

_____

_____

_____

_____

_____

_____

_____

_____

_____

_____

_____

_____

_____

_____

_____

_____

_____

_____

_____

Week 6

Love

Pillar #5 - Leadership is Loving People

Day 1 - Child of God, Loved by God

Commit to reading and memorizing 1 John 3:1, *"See what great love the Father has lavished on us, that we should be called children of God! And that is what we are!"* You are a child of God, loved by God. Let me repeat that. *You are a child of God, loved by God.* As you let that sink in, listen to the song, "Who You Say I Am" by Hillsong Worship (Fielding, B., Morgan, R., 2018). Draw close to God every day by taking the vertical love of God and passing it horizontally to the people around you—in your home, your work, your community, and to the strangers passing by. 1 John 4:11 says, "Dear friends, since God so loved us, we also ought to love one another." Go and love one another.

Day 2 - Examine Yourself

Insert your name into the following sentences.

Sentence #1 - _____ _ is an efficient leader who always has their head down, checking off their to-do lists and finishing projects.

Sentence #2 - _____ is a loving leader who always has their head up, looking around to the needs of others, ready and willing to show Christ's love to the people around them.

How would people describe you? Like the leader in sentence one with their head down, missing the needs of others around them? Or

169

like the leader in sentence two with their head up showing Christ's love to those around them? As a friend once told me, "Move at the speed of love." Be prepared to make daily sacrifices for the good of others.

Day 3 - Be Patient

Patience is often in short supply in our world. Proverbs 14:29 says, "A patient man has great understanding, but a quick-tempered man displays folly." Be intentional about showing God's love to others by patiently responding to *every* situation. Pray that God would provide you with His never-ending supply of patience when it's needed most. We must be patient, bearing with one another in love (Ephesians 4:2).

Day 4 - Be Kind

Ephesians 4:32 says, "Be kind and compassionate to one another, forgiving each other, just as in Christ God forgave you. Pray that God would continue to work on your heart to love others by treating them kindly. Focus on two things today:

1. Surprise someone with an unexpected random act of kindness.
2. Choose to respond with kindness to those who are unkind to you.

Day 5 - Be Humble

Commit to humbly serving others in God's love today. When the hour drew near for Jesus to face death on the cross, he washed his disciple's feet. John 13 tells us that Jesus got up from the meal, wrapped a towel around his waist, poured water into a basin, and began washing his disciple's feet (v.4-5). No matter what you face, look for a way to "wash the feet" of those around you today. Choose to deny yourself today and show God's love by serving others today.

Day 6 - Practice the Pause

Philippians 4:5 says, "Let your gentleness be evident to all; the Lord is near. Commit to showing God's love by responding to *every* situation with gentleness. Be aware of tense moments when it could be easy to react harshly to others. Write the following verse on a notecard and keep it by your desk, computer, or mirror: *A gentle answer turns away wrath, but a harsh word stirs up anger* (Proverbs 15:1). Be a leader in your home and work who responds with gentleness to others in *all* situations by how you speak and act. *Practice the pause!*

Day 7 - Rest

Rest in God's unfailing love. Read and reflect on the goodness of God through Psalm 94, verses 18 through 19:

> When I said, "My foot is slipping,"
> Your love, O Lord, supported me.
> When anxiety was great within me,
> Your consolation brought joy to my soul.

Such sweet, sweet words, "Your love, O Lord, supported me." His love is your support when your foot is slipping. His love is your joy when anxiety is great within you. His love, His love, His love...Rejoice in God's unfailing love and commit to growing in love daily.

Week 6 Reflections

_____
_____
_____
_____
_____
_____
_____
_____
_____
_____
_____
_____
_____
_____
_____
_____
_____
_____
_____
_____
_____
_____
_____
_____

Week 7

Encourage

Pillar #6 - Leadership is Encouraging People

Day 1 - Salt and Light

Today, commit to reading and reflecting on these words from Jesus found in Matthew 5:13-16:

"You are the salt of the earth. But if the salt loses its saltiness, how can it be made salty again? It is no longer good for anything, except to be thrown out and trampled underfoot. You are the light of the world. A town built on a hill cannot be hidden. Neither do people light a lamp and put it under a bowl. Instead, they put it on its stand, and it gives light to everyone in the house. In the same way, let your light shine before others, that they may see your good deeds and glorify your Father in heaven."

How can these words from Jesus encourage you to be an encourager?

Day 2 - Write Two Letters to Yourself

You are "fearfully and wonderfully made." Be intentional about writing two letters to yourself as if it's 10 or 20 years from now. Write one letter as if you look back with regret. This letter will focus on poor decisions and the people impacted by those decisions. Next, write the second letter as if the right choices were made. You will reflect on your wise decisions over those 10 or 20 years and the people impacted the most. You can also write letters from your kids' or spouse's perspective as if they were sharing their experiences and memories of their childhood or relationship with you. Lastly, hold on to those letters and refer back to them when necessary.

Day 3 - Bite Your Tongue

Commit to only speaking words that build up and encourage others today. Refrain from any gossip or negative talk. Paul tells us in Ephesians 4:29, "Do not let any unwholesome talk come out of your mouths, but only what is helpful for building others up according to their needs, that it may benefit those who listen."

Before you speak, whether to someone or about someone, are the words about to come out of your mouth helpful in building others up, or do they tear others down?

An entire forest can be set on fire by a spark and a large ship can be steered by a small rudder (James 3:4-5). The tongue is small, but powerful. Preserve and protect others through your words. Use your tongue to encourage and build others up.

Day 4 - 30 Seconds

Today, pray and ask God to lay someone on your heart who could use a word of encouragement. As a name comes to you, simply take thirty seconds to send them a text message of encouragement, letting them know that you are thinking and praying for them. Add flavor to their life and let God take it from there.

Day 5 - Handwrite It

Today, make the extra effort to encourage someone with a handwritten note. Pray that God would put someone on your heart who could benefit from receiving written words of encouragement. Handwritten notes add an authentic touch to communication, show that you care, and exemplify the human side of leadership.

Day 6 - Celebrate Others

Today, be intentional about noticing and celebrating the work of others. It doesn't have to be anything elaborate. Let others know you see their hard work, they are important to you, and their efforts matter. Encourage others by showing them that they are valued and appreciated. A simple "Thank you" and "Well done" can go a long way in encouraging others. Someone in your life may need to hear four simple words: "I'm proud of you."

Day 7 - Rest

Today, rest in knowing you serve a God who is the light of the world. He is where your light comes from. Jesus said in John 8:12, "I am the light of the world. Whoever follows me will not walk in darkness, but will have the light of life." Not only does Jesus say He is the light of the world, but He also tells us that *we* are the light of the world. What a great compliment and responsibility to serve as God's ambassadors, living as light in a dark and hurting world. Rest in him.

Week 7 Reflections

_____

_____

_____

_____

_____

_____

_____

_____

_____

_____

_____

_____

_____

_____

_____

_____

_____

_____

_____

_____

_____

Closing Prayer

This book will end differently than any other book you've read. I'm going to close this book in prayer. As you read the prayer, please know that this is my heartfelt prayer for you as a leader.

Heavenly Father,

As leaders, you have called us to a tremendous task of leading others: our spouses, children, friends, co-workers, employees, strangers, and anyone we cross paths with—each one of them "running their own race" that you marked out for them. What a tremendous opportunity to serve you and to serve others!

You are the vine; we are your branches. If we remain in you, we will bear much fruit; apart from you, we can do nothing. You are the source of all true life and nourishment. The only way we can grow and be fruitful, both individually and for others, is by staying vitally connected to you. Help us, Father; we cannot do it on our own.

I pray you would equip us to lead with a heart for PEOPLE.

*A heart that **Prioritizes** people*
*A heart that **Empathizes** with people*
*A heart that **Observes** the needs of others and responds with compassion*
*A heart that **Prays** for and with people*
*A heart that **Loves** people*
*And a heart that **Encourages** people.*

Heavenly Father, when we recognize it is You we are leading with and for, we can see differently, and we can lead differently. Strengthen us to be your hands and feet, to be salt and light to others. When we see and lead people through **Your** *lens and with* **Your** *strength, there is no limit to the transformation that can take place across our homes, families, schools, businesses, and organizations.*

Of course, Father God, we, as branches, must be connected to you, the vine, for a fruitful impact on others. An impact that stretches far beyond what our finite minds can comprehend. Prepare us right now to be the leaders you want us to be in all areas of our life. Most importantly, may YOU be glorified in our leadership!

God, You Lead, we will follow.

In Jesus' name I pray, Amen.

References

Angelou, M. (n.d.). Goodreads. Retrieved February 2, 2023, from https://www.goodreads.com/quotes/663523-at-the-end-of-the-day-people-won-t-remember-what

Bauermaster, Z. (2022). *Leading with a humble heart: A 40-day devotional for leaders.* ConnectEDD.

Beihl, B., Redmon, J., Shirk, J., Weaver, M. (2015). My story. [Recorded by Weaver, M.]. On *Beautiful Offerings*. Fervent.

Brown, C., Furtick, S., Hammer, T., Lake, B. (2020). Graves into gardens. [Recorded by Lake B, and Elevation Worship} On *Graves Into Gardens*. Sony Music Nashville/Elevation Worship.

Carnegie, D. (1936). *How to win friends and influence people.* Simon and Schuster.

Carnes, C., Maher, M., Jackson., R. (2019). Run to the father. [Recorded by Maher, Mt.]. *On Run to the Father.* Sparrow (SPR).

Case, J., Helser, J., Johnson, B. (2015). No longer slaves. [Recorded by Helser, D., and Helser, J.]. *On We Will Not Be Shaken.* Bethel Music.

Collins Dictionary. (n.d.). *Overflow.* In Collinsdictionary.com

Covey, S. M. R. (2008). *The speed of trust.* Simon & Schuster.

Dixon, C. (2023) Build a boat. [Recorded by Dixon, C]. On *Canvas*. Atlantic.

Dungy, T., & Whitaker, N. (2011). *The mentor leader.* Tyndale House Publishers.

Fielding, B., Morgan, R. (2018). Who you say I am. [Recorded by Hillsong Worship]. On *There is More*. Hillsong Music Capitol CMG.

Greenway, T. (2015, November 9). *Truett Cathy's unexpected approach to business and life.*

Hayes, W. (2018). Craig. [Recorded by Hayes, W.]. On *Boom*. Monument.

Hayes, W. (2021). Fancy like. [Recorded by Hayes, W.]. On *Country Stuff the Album*. Monument Nashville.

Heath, B., Ingram, J. (2008). Give me your eyes. [Recorded by Heath, B.]. On *What if We*. Reunion.

Ironside, H. A. (n.d). Goodreads. Retrieved February 3, 2023, from https://www.goodreads.com/quotes/189180-we-would-worry-less-if-we-praised-more-thanksgiving-is

Leaf, C. (2022, April 17). *This one common thing could be damaging your brain*. Dr. Leaf.

Lemmel, H. (1922). Turn your eyes upon jesus. Glad Songs.

Lewis, C. S. (n.d.). Quotefancy. Retrieved February 3, 2023 from https://quotefancy.com/quote/5580/C-S-Lewis-Integrity-is-doing-the-right-thing-even-when-no-one-is-watching

Luther, M. (n.d.) Goodreads. Retrieved February 3, 2023 from https://www.goodreads.com/quotes/35269-i-have-so-much-to-do-that-i-shall-spend

Mathis, D. (2015, April 16). *Jesus wept*. Desiring God.

McWilliams, L. (2021, October 14). *New EY Consulting Survey confirms 90% of US workers believe empathetic leadership leads to higher job satisfaction and 79% agree it decreases employee turnover*. EY.

Merriam Webster. (n.d.) *Byproduct*. In Merriam-webster.com.

Merriam Webster. (n.d.) *Overcommit*. In Merriam-webster.com.

Odetta, H. (1962). This little light of mine. [Recorded by Odetta, H]. On *Odetta Singing Folks Song*.

Oxford Learner's Dictionaries. (n.d) *With*. In Oxfordlearner'sdictionaries.com.

Oxford Learner's Dictionaries. (n.d). *Foundation*. In Oxfordlearner'sdictionaries.com.

Oxford Learner's Dictionaries. (n.d). *Precious*. In Oxfordlearner'sdictionaries.com.

Oxford Learner's Dictionaries. (n.d). *Perspective*. In Oxfordlearner'sdictionaries.com.

Oxford Learner's Dictionaries. (n.d). *Treasure*. In Oxfordlearner'sdictionaries.com.

Rath, T., & Conchie, B. (2008). *Strengths based leadership: Great leaders, teams, and why people follow.* Gallup Press.

Sinach. (2015). Waymaker. [Recorded by Sinach]. On *Waymaker- Live.*

Sproul, R.C. (n.d.). Goodreads. Retrieved February 3, 2023, from https://www.goodreads.com/quotes/1152012-the-word-of-god-can-be-in-the-mind-without

Spurgeon, C. (n.d.). Sermon Quotes. Retrieved February 3, 2023, from https://sermonquotes.com/authors/9140-no-one-ever-outgrows.html

Spurgeon, C. H. (1881, September 4). *Love's labours by C. H. Spurgeon.* Blue Letter Bible.

Spurgeon, C.H. (1873, April 27). *The light of the world.* The Spurgeon Center.

Spurgeon, C. H. (2018). Morning and evening: Daily readings. Wilder Publications, LLC.

Taylor, M. (2022). *The noble school leader: The five-square approach to leading schools with emotional intelligence.* Jossey-Bass.

Theodore Roosevelt quote: "comparison is the thief of joy." Quotefancy. (n.d.).

Tripp, P. (2014, April 23). *Questions.* PaulTripp.com.

Tripp , P. (2017, February 15). *23 things that love is.* PaulTripp.com.

Tripp , P. (2021, August 30). *018. A case study of the heart.* PaulTripp.com.

Understanding the meaning of compassion. What Is Compassion? Understanding The Meaning of Compassion. (n.d.).

Voskamp, A. (2014). *Unwrapping the greatest gift: A family celebration of christmas.* Tyndale House Publishers, Inc.

Warren, R. (2002) *The purpose driven life: What on earth I am here for?* Zondervan 2002.

Ziglar, T. (n.d) *You don't build a business.* Ziglar Inc.

Zondervan. (2009). *Holy bible: New international version.*

About the Author

Zac Bauermaster is an educational leader passionate about people. He serves as Principal of Providence Elementary School located in Lancaster County, Pennsylvania. His leadership style exemplifies a people-first approach as he seeks to glorify God in all he does. Zac's first book, *Leading with a Humble Heart: A 40-Day Devotional for Leaders*, was published by ConnectEDD Publishing in

July of 2022. He is passionate about encouraging people to grow as leaders inside and outside of their homes as they run with perseverance the race marked out for them (Hebrews 12:1). Most importantly, Zac is a husband to his wife Carly, and father to three young kids: Olivia, Eliot, and Isaac. Zac is a firm believer in leading his family first. The family resides in Lancaster County, Pennsylvania. You can connect with Zac at: www.zacbauermaster.com.

More from ConnectEDD Publishing

Since 2015, ConnectEDD has worked to transform education by empowering educators to become better-equipped to teach, learn, and lead. What started as a small company designed to provide professional learning events for educators has grown to include a variety of services to help educators and administrators address essential challenges. ConnectEDD offers instructional and leadership coaching, professional development workshops focusing on a variety of educational topics, a roster of nationally recognized educator associates who possess hands-on knowledge and experience, educational conferences custom-designed to meet the specific needs of schools, districts, and state/national organizations, and ongoing, personalized support, both virtually and onsite. In 2020, ConnectEDD expanded to include publishing services designed to provide busy educators with books and resources consisting of practical information on a wide variety of teaching, learning, and leadership topics. Please visit us online at connecteddpublishing.com or contact us at: info@connecteddpublishing.com

Recent Publications:

Live Your Excellence: Action Guide by Jimmy Casas

Culturize: Action Guide by Jimmy Casas

Daily Inspiration for Educators: Positive Thoughts for Every Day of the Year by Jimmy Casas

Eyes on Culture: Multiply Excellence in Your School by Emily Paschall

Pause. Breathe. Flourish. Living Your Best Life as an Educator by William D. Parker

L.E.A.R.N.E.R. Finding the True, Good, and Beautiful in Education by Marita Diffenbaugh

Educator Reflection Tips Volume II: Refining Our Practice by Jami Fowler-White

Handle With Care: Managing Difficult Situations in Schools with Dignity and *Respect* by Jimmy Casas and Joy Kelly

Disruptive Thinking: Preparing Learners for Their Future by Eric Sheninger

Permission to be Great: Increasing Engagement in Your School by Dan Butler

Daily Inspiration for Educators: Positive Thoughts for Every Day of the Year, *Volume II* by Jimmy Casas

The 6 Literacy Levers: Creating a Community of Readers by Brad Gustafson

The Educator's ATLAS: Your Roadmap to Engagement by Weston Kieschnick

In This Season: Words for the Heart by Todd Nesloney, LaNesha Tabb, Tanner Olson, and Alice Lee

Leading with a Humble Heart: A 40-Day Devotional for Leaders by Zac Bauermaster

Recalibrate the Culture: Our Why...Our Work...Our Values by Jimmy Casas

Creating Curious Classrooms: The Beauty of Questions by Emma Chiappetta

Crafting the Culture: 45 Reflections on What Matters Most by Joe Sanfelippo and Jeffrey Zoul

Improving School Mental Health: The Thriving School Community Solution by Charle Peck and Dr. Cameron Caswell

Building Authenticity: A Blueprint for the Leader Inside You by Todd Nesloney And Tyler Cook

Connecting Through Conversation: A Playbook for Talking with Kids by Erika Bare and Tiffany Burns

The Dream Factory: Designing a Purposeful Life by Mark Trumbo

Stories Behind Stances: Creating Empathy Through Hearing "The Other Side" by Chris Singleton

Happy Eyes: All Things to All People by Ryan Tillman

The Generative Age Artificial Intelligence and the Future of Education by Alana Winnick

Recalibrate the Culture: Action Guide by Jimmy Casas

Printed in Great Britain
by Amazon

36326290R00115